CRACKING

THE

SALES

MANAGEMENT

CODE

**The Secrets to Measuring and Managing
SALES PERFORMANCE**

JASON JORDAN

WITH
MICHELLE VAZZANA

New York   Chicago   San Francisco   Lisbon   London   Madrid   Mexico City
Milan   New Delhi   San Juan   Seoul   Singapore   Sydney   Toronto

Copyright © 2012 by Vantage Point Performance, Inc. All rights reserved. Printed in the United States of America. Except as permitted under the United States Copyright Act of 1976, no part of this publication may be reproduced or distributed in any form or by any means, or stored in a database or retrieval system, without the prior written permission of the publisher.

9 10 11 12 13 14 15   QFR/QFR   1 9 8 7 6 5 4

ISBN   978-0-07-176573-2
MHID   0-07-176573-5

e-ISBN   978-0-07-176961-7
e-MHID   0-07-176961-7

Library of Congress Cataloging-in-Publication Data

Jordan, Jason, 1970-
    Cracking the sales management code : the secrets to measuring and managing sales performance / by Jason Jordan, Michelle Vazzana
        p. cm.
    ISBN-13: 978-0-07-176573-2 (alk. paper)
    ISBN-10: 0-07-176573-5 (alk. paper)
    1. Sales management.   I. Vazzana, Michelle   II. Title.
    HF5438.4.J67 2012
    658.8'72—dc23

                                                        2011018021

Interior design by THINK Book Works

McGraw-Hill books are available at special quantity discounts to use as premiums and sales promotions or for use in corporate training programs. To contact a representative, please e-mail us at bulksales@mcgraw-hill.com.

Contents

PART 3

Using the Code to Manage *Your* Sales Force

Foreword

In the good old days, when selling was so much simpler, it was widely put about that sales success rested on the "three Ss" of good selling:

Selection: recruiting really high-potential salespeople
Strategy: helping them make insightful sales plans for each account
Skill: teaching them how to make effective sales calls

If you could get those three things right, then you had all you needed for a world-beating sales force.

At a conference in Europe last year, someone asked me whether I thought the three Ss still applied to the much more sophisticated sales environment of today. I answered that, yes, selection, strategy, and skill remain valid predictors of sales success. Really good people are still scarcer than gold, and if you can select the best, you are an automatic winner. Strategy and skill are just as essential to success as ever they were—although both have become more sophisticated in recent years. The questioner frowned at my response, and I could see that I had disappointed her. I hope she reads this, because I'd like her to know that, after the conference, her frown prompted me to do some deeper thinking about her question. If I had to bet on the three most important factors for sales success today, would I still put my money on the three Ss? Or has the revolution in selling that we've seen over the last 10 years so changed our understanding of sales success that there are now newer and more important factors?

I certainly don't want to underestimate the importance of selection, skill, or strategy. They remain essential ingredients to the success of any sales force. But it's increasingly clear that they are no longer enough. In recent years I've worked with some sales forces that have had good offerings, good salespeople, decent account planning, and an above-average level of skill compared with their competition. According to the three Ss, these sales forces should have a superior performance. Yet, in many cases, they were losing market share to the competition. Why? What did competitors have that was making them more successful? In some cases it wasn't a sales force issue. The competitor had superior pricing or marketing, a dynamic culture, or a distribution advantage. But, in more instances than I would have liked, a sales force strong on the three Ss of selection, strategy, and skill was being outsold.

I've pondered mightily on these cases, with the kind of thinking that you do late at night when there's a niggling issue troubling you and you can't sleep. After all, I made my name in the field of sales skill and sales strategy, so it wasn't easy to challenge a foundation of my own reputation. But, after much agonizing, I came up with my finalists. If I had to pick just three components of success in the new sales world, I would choose the three Ms:

Management, especially first-line sales supervision
Metrics that go beyond the usual activity-based measurement
Methodology, or working with a systematic and disciplined approach

Let's look more closely at each one to see why these three are the essential components of sales success for the immediate future. And, at this point, I should add that *Cracking the Sales Management Code* is all about the three Ms of management, metrics, and methodology.

MANAGEMENT

In my embarrassingly long career, I must have worked closely with more than 50 sales forces in an effort to significantly improve their performance. I think it's fair to say that I've generally been successful in turning around poor-performing sales forces if the first-line managers I worked with had good potential, even if the salespeople themselves were mediocre. But I've never succeeded, even with half-decent salespeople, when it was the other way around. If first-line managers were of low caliber, no amount of effort, no reorganization, no training made any sustainable difference. For the last 10 years, whenever I've been asked to help turn around a sales force, my first questions are always about the capability and potential of sales supervisors and managers. So selection, one of the old "three Ss," is still a vital component of success. But in the ever more complex business environment where companies must compete for the future, it's even more important to select good sales managers than good salespeople.

However, the sales management problem doesn't end with the recruitment or promotion of talented people. There are many thousands of bright high-potential sales managers who are highly motivated to succeed and who are nevertheless struggling to survive. They are ready and willing to do the right thing. What they lack is help and advice on what to do. They can't rely on older, experienced managers within their companies who generally learned the sales business in the days when the definition of strategy was "simple tactics ruthlessly executed." And, unfortunately, many of these outdated senior managers are forcefully urging their juniors to do too many of the wrong things. Where can new managers turn for advice? If they were salespeople, they could go to the 5,000 or more books that give advice on how to sell. But, as we know all too well from the sad history of outstanding salespeople who have been promoted into becoming abysmal sales managers, selling and sales management are entirely different things. So what can the new manager read that's helpful? By my count, there are less than a hundred books on sales management, more than half of them out of print. Worse, many of the available books are general guides on how to manage people, just putting the word *sales* in front of the word *manager*. There's an acute shortage of good books on the specifics of sales management. That's why I encouraged Jason to write *Cracking the Sales Management Code*.

It's about the practical specifics of sales management in the new era—and it fills a void.

What are some of these specifics? Let me give a few examples. There's advice on what CRM (customer relationship management) can do and, even more important, what it can't do. There's a clear explanation of the steps needed to link sales activities to business results; there are practical tools to help sales managers wade through the deepening flood of control issues that come with increasing sales complexity. These are important and useful topics, and sales managers will welcome the advice that this book offers.

METRICS

I'm often asked by clients, "What one thing do my sales managers need to understand better?" "Metrics," I invariably reply. Perhaps the most misunderstood of all sales management activity is the design and use of metrics. The great scientist Lord Kelvin wrote, almost two centuries ago, "If you cannot measure it, if you cannot express it in quantitative terms, then your knowledge is of a meager and insubstantial kind." That, in a nutshell, is the justification for sales metrics. What you cannot measure, you cannot improve. Sales metrics are important because they allow us to measure, understand, control, and improve the performance of sales forces. But what does *metrics* mean to the average sales manager? Chances are that the word conjures up visions of activity management, measures such as call reports or calls per day, tracking of targets and quotas in terms of volume, and profitability per salesperson. These are the tried and true metrics of the old selling. *Cracking the Sales Management Code* convincingly argues that these classic measures are not only inadequate but, for most sales forces today, can be downright unhelpful.

Jason, Michelle, and their colleagues, working with that excellent organization the Sales Education Foundation, identified 306 metrics that were being used by the sales forces in their survey. That, you might agree, adds up to a whole cartload of metrics. How do you see the wood from the trees in this smorgasbord of more than 300 choices? (Or, to avoid my ghastly mixed metaphor, perhaps I should ask, "Where's the beef in this feast of choices?") The main theme of this book is how to answer that question—what it takes to get the right metrics, how to select them, how to test them, and how to use them to run a high-performing sales force. I shan't say more about the new metrics here because I wouldn't want to intrude on the clear story that Jason lays out. But I would urge serious sales managers to invest time to thoroughly understand the important role played by metrics—and this book is a good place to start. The future will bring even more exciting developments in sales metrics. Companies like GE are already experimenting with Six Sigma metrics, and a fundamental understanding of measurement in these companies is a foundation skill for management success.

METHODOLOGY

The final *M* in my three new pillars of sales success is *methodology*. I choose the word because it's a wide enough term to cover a range of methods, tools, and techniques that can be used to bring order and predictability to selling. The two most common forms of sales methodology are sales process—or its simpler versions, called *pipelines* or *funnels*—and CRM systems. The purpose of a sales process is to break down the sales cycle into sequential steps and to track the progress of each sales opportunity as it moves through the steps. Each step has a range of activities and measures associated with it that must be completed before moving to the next step. In this way, sales forecasts can become more accurate, and managers can diagnose and intervene when important opportunities need their help and guidance. That much is Sales 101. Almost everyone today has some form of sales methodology to organize and systematize their selling activity. Companies have spent many billions on sales process and CRM systems, generally with feeble and disappointing results. Partly this disappointment has come from overselling of what CRM can do by software vendors whose understanding of sales sometimes borders on the nonexistent. But the companies who bought systems that failed to deliver on promises must shoulder some of the blame. They naively expected that the system would magically solve most of their problems and, with very few exceptions, failed to understand the enormous difficulty and hard work involved in implementing a sales methodology.

I go through all of this to explain why sales methodologies are often seen cynically by practicing sales managers. And that's a pity. In today's world, the success of a sales force may depend more on having a good sales methodology than on any other factor. One of the reasons I think *Cracking the Sales Management Code* makes such a useful contribution is that it takes a sensible and balanced view of sales methodology. It avoids both the breathless enthusiasm of the CRM junkies and the unwarranted cynicism of the detractors who have been victims of bad process and are revenging themselves in print. Such a balance is hard to find.

So read this book. It will give you practical help with all three pillars of the new selling—management, metrics, and methodology. And I wish you every success in applying the ideas to your selling.

Neil Rackham

PART 1

Metrics, Metrics Everywhere

CRM, Reporting, and a False Sense of Control

CHAPTER 1

THE WAR ROOM

So there we were. The war room.

Our Fortune 100 client was showing us the sequestered confer-ence room where the company's senior leadership gathers weekly to review business performance and set strategic direction. On the walls hung a sea of performance reports showing everything from current financial projections to the number of customer-facing calls the sales force had conducted year-to-date. Literally hundreds of data points culled from the company's customer relationship management (CRM) tool were reported in vividly colored charts for the leadership team's real-time consideration.

There was data at an aggregate level. Data at the sales man-ager level. Data sliced by product line. Data sliced by region, by customer segment, and by the stages of the company's sales cycle. Data sliced and diced in every way imaginable—truly a world-class demonstration of performance reporting. It was a scene that would make any IT director stare in amazement and any senior executive turn green with envy.

Looking at the walls, it was easy to envision a typical weekly war room meeting, which might resemble the classic scene from a World War II Hollywood movie in which analysts scurry about updating information on the walls, while leadership takes it all in and formulates a strategy to outflank the enemy. Except in this case, the generals are VPs of sales. The soldiers are salespeople. The battlefields are sales territories. The numbers on the wall are not enemy head count—they are product sales, pipeline size, sales rep activity, win/loss ratios, profit margins, and of course, revenue forecasts. Anything and everything that can be reported has a spot reserved on the war room walls.

The constantly updated numbers are key ingredients for the primary activity in the war room—to quickly identify trends (both good and bad) and dole out urgent directives to the field. Is the pipeline too small? Then have the salespeople do more prospecting. Profit margins down? Tell the sales managers to hold their ground. Forecasts inaccurate? Have the reps update the data more frequently. No doubt these weekly meetings are intense, focused, and perceived as high-impact. Ah, the war room. Who wouldn't want one?

This was not the first war room we had seen in a sales force. Several years ago, while conducting some research into sales management best practices, we encountered another similar lair. In true best-practice style, this leadership team even had military paraphernalia spread about the room. Reams of paper lined the walls displaying everything from territory coverage plans to benchmark performance data. Sales, it would appear, is a battlefield.

Most companies have their own scaled-down version of the war room—at least in spirit, if not in practice. They have a set of reports that they regularly examine to assess progress against their goals and to determine what actions must be taken in order to ensure the goals are met. The reports aren't always large-format color prints with pie charts, bar graphs, and scatter diagrams, but it is exceedingly rare today to find a sales force of any size that hasn't invested in some type of customer relationship management (CRM) or sales force automation (SFA) software for the primary purpose of increased reporting.[1]

---

1. For the purposes of simplicity, we will use the broader term *customer relationship management (CRM)*, which typically includes sales force automation functionality.

In fact, we can't recall working with any sales force in the past decade that didn't have technology supporting at least a portion of its activities. CRM tools have become pervasive and will continue to grow in importance as technology integrates with an increasing percentage of our daily activities. This will in turn enable even greater reporting at increasingly granular levels of detail. Soon the battlefield will be perfectly in focus for sales management to view.

GOT CONTROL?

So what has all this reporting gotten us? Well, having all this data at our fingertips has become like comfort food for leadership. A real-time view of sales force performance makes us feel in touch with the organization. And increased transparency to field-level activities gives us the satisfying sense that we are somehow in control of the sales force's behaviors. However, visibility to an action does not equate to control over it. Let us give you an example of the life-threatening danger of this assumption.

When one of the my children was 18 months old, I left her with a babysitter while I made a quick trip to the store (I was no doubt as much in search of silence as I was in search of provisions). When I returned to my house and opened the door, I saw the terrifying sight of my precious child standing upright on a steep set of stairs, wobbling in her attempt to make it to the next step. Meanwhile the babysitter was sitting calmly across the room just watching the situation unfold. Witnessing the obvious terror on my face as I sprinted across the room toward the teetering child, the sitter attempted to calm me down by saying, "Don't worry. I am right here. I can see everything she's doing." Trying only halfheartedly to contain my anger, I responded, "*Watching* my daughter fall to her death is not the same thing as *preventing* her from falling to her death."

Similarly, watching the walls of the war room is not the same as directing the battle on the field. While seeing activity-level data such as Number of Calls Made or Percentage of Customers Contacted creates a sense of participation in the activities, in reality, it is more akin to watching salespeople climb treacherous stairs from across the room hoping they don't fall to their deaths. You can see the disaster happen, but you can't control the outcome.

Despite the billions of dollars that have been spent to enable deep and wide reporting of sales force activities and outcomes, we have seen few instances of increased reporting capabilities actually leading to greater control over sales force performance. Greater visibility provides you with exactly that—greater visibility. Not greater control.

But before we gain a reputation as report haters, let us state clearly that we *love* good data. In fact, we would argue that it is impossible to manage successfully in today's sophisticated selling environment without reliable data to assess current performance, analyze events, uncover trends, and provide actionable direction to a sales force. It's just that despite all the analysis and discussion taking place in the war room, we all too often see the same directive emerge: "Field, do more."

Call on more customers, put more opportunities in the pipeline, close more deals—it's as though all things can be solved by simply asking for "more." It's somewhat concerning that given the highly sophisticated analytic capabilities that CRM affords us, very little direction is given back to sales managers and their reps other than to do more. The "do more" mantra may feel like exerting control, but it would be somewhat like telling my 18-month-old, "Don't trip." She wouldn't know what it meant, and the eventual (and potentially tragic) outcome would be left to chance.

THE SOURCE OF THE PROBLEM

In a nutshell, here is where we are.

Over the last 20 years, we have witnessed a technological revolution known as CRM. With few limits, we now have the ability to generate extremely detailed reports that allow us to see both the activities of our sales reps and the outcomes they create.

The amount of information that we have to help us manage is unprecedented in the history of sales management and is only getting bigger. Our challenge in the future is more likely to be an excess of data, not a scarcity of it. Even today, we observe "analysis paralysis" in companies for which information overload has crippled the very decision-making ability that reporting was meant to enable.

So with all this information at our fingertips, we are little more able to proactively influence sales force performance than we were billions of dollars ago. We are more enlightened about what's happened—and even what is currently happen*ing*—but we have little more control over the future than we did in the past. What then are we missing?

What we are missing is quite fundamental:

> **We are missing the operating instructions for a sales force.**

How do the numbers on the war room wall *work*? Of all the data points that we see on our reports, which are the inputs, and which are the outputs? Which are the causes, and which are the effects? If I want to move this number, should I push that one or pull another? What we don't yet know is *how to work the numbers*.

If we did understand the relationships between all the numbers on the wall, then we could exert more control over them. Want more revenue? No problem—do this. Want more new customers? No worries—do that. This is the level of understanding that sales leaders do not have today. Instead, management concludes: Want more revenue? Do more. Want more customers? Do more. But sometimes the revenue and customers don't come.

This is where CRM has left us. It has given us the power to *see* what the sales force is doing, but it didn't come with instructions for what to do with that newfound visibility. We can get plenty of data from the magnificent reporting machine, but we haven't been told how to use it. Basically, our ability to report data accelerated faster than our ability to understand it. For better or worse, we cracked the CRM programming code *before* we cracked the sales management code.

HOW SALES HAS TRAILED ITS PEERS

Sales is unlike its corporate peers finance, manufacturing, and marketing in many ways. And as patrons of the sales function, we think it is not only different but also better. We could argue that it's more dynamic, more exciting, more challenging, more fun, and outright more important than its organizational siblings, but there is one place that sales has woefully trailed other business disciplines: discipline itself.

During the nineteenth and twentieth centuries, every other corporate function developed a body of knowledge that enabled it to measure and manage itself in a more consistent and predictable way. Consequently, corporate functions other than sales enjoy a fundamental understanding of their inner workings, and they are able to direct their day-to-day business with confidence toward their ultimate objectives.

Finance has a robust set of metrics with clearly understood implications. Any financial professional can easily analyze and discuss the relationships among income statements, balance sheets, and statements of cash flow. They have universal standards such as the generally accepted accounting principles (GAAP) that provide a common language with which to manage their business. They have a discipline.

Manufacturing too has a rich set of management frameworks that it uses to control and direct its outputs. Any plant manager can easily recite standard measures such as throughput, defects, quality, and cost while intuitively understanding the trade-offs of improving one versus the other. They have programs such as total quality management (TQM) and Six Sigma that guide them to higher levels of performance. They have a discipline.

Marketing was one of the last business functions to accept accountability and embrace a strict discipline of measurement and management. Nonetheless, marketers have long understood and used key management concepts such as customer segmentation, market share, customer profitability, and profit margin to make decisions and gauge success. If nothing else, one can measure marketing's professional legitimacy by its prevalence as a major in our colleges and universities. It has a discipline.

Note that the development of GAAP, TQM, and other frameworks used to manage our functional peers developed well before the advent of the computer. They were created as their leadership recognized a need for structured thinking and a common language to diagnose business issues and implement proactive change. When information systems fully blossomed in the late twentieth century, their business functions became more efficient to manage, but the underlying operating instructions remained constant. Other business functions had already cracked their management code, and information technology just made their jobs easier.

And then there is sales.

Sales has somehow evaded the management rigor and professional discipline that has burgeoned in its peer groups. There is no sales equivalent of GAAP. There is no standard TQM framework for sales improvement. And there are currently fewer than 50 colleges and universities in the United States that offer a major or minor in sales. Compared to finance, manufacturing, or marketing, the discipline of sales is still in its infancy.

So when information technology eventually came to the sales force, there was relatively little to automate. Sales had no formal operating instructions for itself. In contrast to its organizational peers, sales' information systems were just layered on top of unstructured processes and inconsistent execution. Basically, sales forces automated their own forms of chaos.

Rather than beginning their automation projects by defining and mapping formal selling processes, sales forces began by designing reports. Rather than asking how the technology should support their critical selling activities, sales forces assumed that the technology had its own inherent value. (One of our past clients even confessed that its deliberate CRM implementation strategy was to *first* get the technology deployed and *then* worry about defining the processes. Two years later, there we were . . . helping the client add structure to its automated chaos.)

We strongly believe this is the reason that CRM has failed to create a more controlled sales environment. It's not that CRM's expectations were overblown, nor that its implementation was botched. Senior leadership watched as technology revolutionized finance, manufacturing, and even marketing, so it was completely reasonable to expect a similar revolution in sales.

But the revolution didn't occur. It didn't occur because unlike our organizational peers before us, sales did not have a fully cooked management discipline. We had all of the pieces to the puzzle, but the overall picture had not yet come into focus. We had not cracked the sales management code.

This book makes one big step toward establishing a rigorous sales management discipline. Based on our research into how leading companies use metrics to manage their sales forces, we have developed a management system that will predictably link the activities in the war room to the battle on the field. It will help sales managers floating in a sea of data to focus their attention on the few metrics that really matter. It will help sales executives to drive their sales forces with a clear set of operating instructions. It will provide a framework for improved sales performance reporting. It will finally crack the sales management code.

PART 2

The Sales Management Code . . . Cracked!

What Can We Really Manage?

CHAPTER 2

Though we open this book with a narrative on CRM and performance metrics, the core issue here is neither technology nor reporting—the core issue is sales management. The advent of information systems and reporting capabilities merely exposed the underlying reality that sales management has not evolved into the discipline it needs to be. We believe this lack of development at the sales management level is in part the by-product of a myopic obsession with developing our frontline sellers. This intense focus on developing salespeople rather than sales managers has been enabled by at least two faulty assumptions.

GREAT SELLERS EVOLVE INTO GREAT MANAGERS . . . MAYBE?

First, there seems to be an assumption that if companies invest enough in developing good salespeople, that same investment will in time yield qualified sales managers. Stated differently, leadership spends lavishly to train its sellers yet ceases to invest in their ongoing development once the sellers are promoted into management. Look at any sales organization, and there is most certainly a budget to train its salespeople. However, with almost equal certainty, there will be no budget to train its sales managers.

One could offer many justifications for this, but it demonstrates a very clear belief that talented salespeople are qualified to seamlessly transform into competent managers. Let us mention one particular skill gap we observe in sales managers that highlights the folly of this belief.

We've had many heated conversations during our careers about whether selling is an art or a science. Regardless of the combatants, we always, of course, reach the conclusion that selling is a combination of both—perhaps even leaning more toward art than science. We've all witnessed superstar sellers who appear to lack the least bit of structure and rigor in their daily activities, yet they are still able to succeed as a result of some chance combination of natural selling ability and proper casting in their sales role. When the right artist gets the right canvas and the right subject to paint, magic can occur.

While it is easy to argue that selling is as much an art as a science, aspiring artists beware: sales *management* is strictly a domain for those with a penchant for science. With extremely rare exception, the best sales managers we've encountered are unconsciously competent scientists. They hold formal meetings with formal agendas on formal schedules. They set rigorous expectations for their salespeople and track progress against those goals with equal rigor. They manage by analysis rather than anecdote and by measurement rather than gut. They are continuous-improvement experts with action plans galore. While their lower-performing peers try to manage with the same artistic flair that served them well as salespeople, high-performing managers adopt a more scientific approach to management that enables them to get consistently higher performance from their team.

Salespeople aren't typically taught management skills, and superstar sellers are legendary for avoiding structure and formality. Yet these are the same people who routinely get promoted into management. Managers do need structure. They do need analytic and critical thinking skills. They do need a management discipline to succeed in their management role. Put simply, preparing salespeople to be great sellers is *not* sufficient preparation for them to become great managers.

The symptoms of this fact have been apparent for decades, but the increasing sophistication of the sales management task has turned it into a serious affliction. Gone are the days when sales management was simply about preparing and motivating your reps to do the same things *you* did before you were promoted into management. Today's sales managers are also expected to be part marketer, part CFO, part IT director, part trainer, and probably parts of a half-dozen other roles. Sales managers are now responsible for segmenting customers, designing territories, setting goals, generating reports, managing information systems, and generally executing their companies' constantly changing go-to-market strategies. We believe that the sales manager's role in the twenty-first century is the most diverse of any in any company, and we strongly contend that the investment being made in its development is not appropriately large.

IT'S THE SALES MANAGER, STUPID

The second assumption that has hindered a focus on sales manager development is the perception that salespeople themselves are the primary agents of sales success. Prevailing wisdom says that given the choice between training salespeople and training sales managers, it is wiser to invest in the frontline sellers. They are the ones who conduct the actual customer-facing activities and whose increased skill should translate directly into increased sales, right? The closer to the action the person is, the more critical his abilities *must* be.

However, we are beginning to see a tidal shift in the way executives view the drivers of improved sales performance. While investing in the skills of frontline salespeople will always be a key to success in the marketplace, the role of the sales manager is now viewed by many as an even greater point of leverage. In fact, many of our clients now look back in despair at how little they've invested in this critical role. Sales managers are often the only contact remote or home-based salespeople have with their organization. They are the primary source of reinforcement for any training or other change effort aimed at the salespeople and are the main channel of communication between executive leadership and the front line. Without sales managers who can effectively influence and direct field salespeople, the generals in the war room have little or no control over the execution of their battle plans.

The realization that leadership has long neglected this critical layer in the sales organization has led to many "aha" moments. We witnessed such an "aha" recently with a client that has roughly 125 sales managers supervising 700 salespeople. The company has a very sophisticated internal training group that invests millions of dollars each year in training its sales force. The client had identified its managers' coaching skills as an area for improvement and asked our firm, Vantage Point Performance, for help. While exploring the nature of the problem, we had a revealing conversation that went almost *exactly* like this:

> **Somewhat Exasperated Director of Training:** *We have trained our salespeople on these activities several times over the years, but the training never seems to stick.*
>
> **Vantage Point Performance:** *What kinds of follow-up have you done to reinforce the training?*
>
> **DoT:** *Well, the sales managers are supposed to be reinforcing the training in the field.*
>
> **VPP:** *So the sales managers have been the primary means of reinforcement for the training that didn't seem to stick?*
>
> **DoT:** *Yes, but for some reason, it just didn't happen.*
>
> **VPP:** *Have the sales managers been present at the salesperson training events?*
>
> **DoT:** *No, we've never had the sales managers present at any of the salesperson training events. In fact, we've intentionally omitted them so the salespeople wouldn't be distracted.*

VPP: *Have you held separate training sessions for the sales managers to educate them on what the salespeople had learned?*

DoT: *No.*

VPP: *Then how are the sales managers supposed to know how to coach the salespeople if they don't attend the salespeople's training or receive a separate training session of their own? How else would they know what they are supposed to be reinforcing?*

DoT: *Well, I guess they wouldn't.* ["Aha" moment.] *I think we may have found the source of the problem.*

VPP: *Well, that's part of the problem—the sales managers certainly need to know what's expected of their salespeople. But even if the managers knew what their salespeople were supposed to be doing, do you think they'd inherently know how to coach and reinforce those behaviors?*

DoT: *No, doing and coaching are two different skill sets. So you're suggesting that we should not only have trained the sales managers along with the salespeople, but additionally we should have trained them on how to reinforce the specific behaviors in the field?*

VPP: *I think that would have been a smart way to protect your investment in your salespeople.*

DoT: [Second "aha" moment] *Yeah, me too.*[1]

As with many companies, our client had made a sizable investment in developing the skills of its salespeople only to ignore the most critical change agent in any sales force, the frontline sales managers. It was not that our client lacked the resources to train its sales managers; it simply didn't realize the importance. Leadership incorrectly assumed that its managers would inherently possess the awareness and ability to reinforce the sales reps' behaviors in the field. Wrong they were.

This was a striking example of how important the sales manager is in driving salesperson effectiveness. If the company had invested in training its sales managers along with its salespeople, the sales reps' new skills might have lasted longer than a few

---

1. Many people reading our client dialogues have expressed disbelief that the conversations took place as described. We assure you that these conversations are not exaggerated for effect. Sometimes reality is stranger than fiction.

hours. Salespeople may be the foot soldiers out fighting the war, but sales managers are the ones equipping them for battle and giving them their marching orders. And an unprepared soldier doesn't stand a fighting chance against a worthy adversary.

Sticking with our war theme, remember the battle cry once used by a political election campaign, "It's the economy, stupid"? The mantra was meant to cut through the multitude of issues and focus campaign staff on what voters perceived as the most painful need of the day—a better economy. Similarly, we would offer our own battle cry to punctuate the most painful need in most sales forces today—well-trained, capable sales managers. We believe that the frontline sales manager is the most powerful point of leverage in any sales force, and providing her with the right training and tools to manage her salespeople will pay dividends far into the future.

CAN YOU MANAGE A NUMBER?

If we agree that the sales manager plays a critical role in driving sales performance, then the next question we might ask is, What can we reasonably expect them to do?

As we discussed, today's sales managers spend hours each week poring over reports that detail the activities and productivity of their salespeople. Additionally, they spend hours each week reviewing those same reports with their sales reps, discussing areas of low performance and brainstorming ways to improve. In many ways, reports have become the primary management tool used in most sales forces. They have taken on a life of their own, and the collections of carefully chosen metrics that are printed on the reports have quietly become the carrots and sticks that motivate and guide the sales force.

Interestingly, there has developed an unstated expectation that sales managers can with enough effort *change* the numbers on the page. There is a tacit understanding that an integral part of a sales manager's role is to make the numbers look right. In fact, we suspect that the phrase "make your number" has become as commonplace in the sales management lexicon as "good morning." It's all about making the number. But can a sales manager truly *make* the numbers? Or phrased differently, can someone with enough willpower and effort actually manage numbers?

When stated in those terms, the answer is obviously no. People can only manage people and resources, not concepts or numbers. However, managers are so often asked to "manage revenue," "manage profit," or "manage" some other metric that they have come to believe it's their responsibility to do so. Managing the numbers has become their de facto job.

Watching sales managers run from meeting to meeting clutching fistfuls of reports began to worry us, as did the vision of leaders gathered in their war rooms formulating battle plans with confidence that their directives to the field would result in better numbers on their walls. Managers are now expected to manage those numbers, and probably hundreds of thousands are desperately trying to do so. In an effort to assess how this management-by-report exercise was being administered more broadly, we decided to explore how leading companies are currently attempting to manage their numbers.

OUR JOURNEY BEGINS

To understand how metrics are being used to manage sales forces, we first partnered with the Sales Education Foundation[2] to survey its corporate constituents. Specifically, we asked sales leaders to provide us with the data points that *they* found the most meaningful in driving the performance of their sales forces. We then expanded the scope of the research to include our own client base, adding data from actual management reports that are being used at both the executive and field levels. In sum, we gathered 306 metrics that are considered by leadership to be the keys to effective sales management. As we began

---

2. The Sales Education Foundation is a not-for-profit organization committed to advancing the profession of sales through increased education and research in colleges and universities. Jason Jordan is a founding board member. Learn more or get involved at http://www.saleseducationfoundation.org.

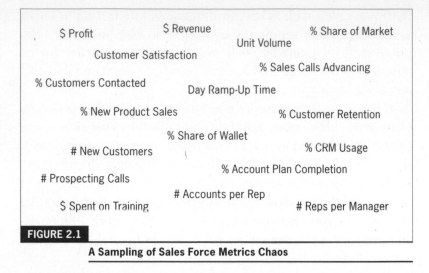

FIGURE 2.1

A Sampling of Sales Force Metrics Chaos

to study the metrics, some very interesting (as well as some very concerning) findings began to emerge.

Foremost, we had hoped that looking across many organizations would allow us to observe a pattern or a common framework for how smart leadership chooses to organize various sales force metrics. Certainly, we thought, companies that had invested millions of dollars in IT infrastructure and spent decades refining their reports would have settled on a best-practice method of categorizing their key performance indicators. Much to the contrary, we found absolute chaos.

One company reported 14 different categories of sales metrics, often with only two metrics per category. Another listed 16 different measures in no particular order whatsoever. One global vice president of sales claimed that he needed only three key numbers to effectively manage his entire sales force. And some responded with terms so vague, it was impossible to immediately discern what they were truly trying to measure (see Figure 2.1).

It was also curious how companies chose to categorize their metrics. Some organized them by business function, reporting measurements on recruiting, training, leadership, technology, and sales processes. Others had a hodgepodge of buckets for their measures, such as revenue, customer satisfaction, forecast accuracy, market segmentation, talent management, or sales pipeline. The company with the most basic structure for its metrics simply chose to divide them into internal and external measures.

But even within one company's set of metrics, the taxonomy often made little sense. For example, customer retention might not be categorized as a measure of customer satisfaction. Or the percentage of a sales rep's time that is spent with customers might be counted as a *cost* to the organization. And measures of revenue tended to show up in categories across the board, like the one company that considered revenue to be both an internal and external measurement. Metrics here, metrics there, literally metrics everywhere.

There are many potential explanations for why the various metrics were arranged (or not) in such a seemingly random fashion. Perhaps it was an artifact of the systems from which they were reported. Or perhaps the different types of measures came from different parts of the organization. And it's equally as likely that the metrics were sorted for reporting to various stakeholders who had slightly different interests. Regardless of the reason we observed such a chaotic mix of sales force metrics, it was quite clear that a best-practice method for categorizing sales metrics had yet to evolve. If we were going to make sense of the relationship between sales management and sales metrics, we would have to do it ourselves.

THE QUESTION

So there we were. Our own war room.

Or at least that's what it resembled with our 306 metrics hanging randomly about the walls. Except that unlike the real war room generals, we were not there to lead—we were there to follow. We were going to follow those seemingly random numbers wherever they would take us, as long as we ended up with a coherent framework of sales force metrics. But how then should we begin our sure-to-be-frustrating journey?

We chose as our tour guide a single question. The question that had led us to this point in time, and the question that would hopefully lead us to crack the sales management code:

[**Can we manage this number?**]

Our first task was to clearly define our use of the term *manage*. What did we mean to say that we could manage a number? Our criterion for *managing* became that a frontline sales manager could directly influence the metric by asking someone to do something differently. That is, he could direct or take some action that would consequently and undoubtedly cause the number to change. No one's consent and no further decisions were required. A sales manager could control that number.

To choose an example of "management" from our everyday lives, we cannot directly manage our children's grades in school. As much as we would like to instruct that B on the report card to become an A, the B is not listening. What we *can* manage, though, is the amount of time that our children spend studying. We can direct our children to study two, three, or even four hours a day in hopes that their grades will ultimately be influenced. The metric of Time Spent Studying is in our control.

Another example would be our physical weight. As wonderful as it would be to step onto the scale and watch that number decrease with ease as we stand there and command, "Lower, lower, lower," in reality, that is a metric we cannot directly manage. We *can* however control how many calories we eat and how frequently we exercise, which should consequently lead to a happier scale-watching experience. Number of Calories Consumed and Hours Spent in Gym are key weight-related metrics that we can directly manage.

As you can see, our task quickly turned into an exercise in separating cause and effect. It became clear that the results of our actions are not as controllable as the actions themselves. There are lots of things in life that we can *influence*, and the ability to influence often feels like the ability to control. However, we can only control or manage the actions of ourselves and, when in a supervisory role, the actions of others. Not surprisingly, we found this to be true in the sales force as well.

And thus began the tedious process of interrogating the metrics on the wall. One by one, we posed to each of them The Question, "Can we manage you?"

> So, Percentage of Time Spent Coaching Reps, we asked, "Can you be managed?" Sure. A manager can allocate more time to coaching.
>
> Number of Sales Calls Made per Rep, "Can you be managed?" Sure. A manager can require more calls by his or her reps. The reps might not want to do it, but that's an issue with compliance, not a problem with the manageability of the metric itself. It's completely reasonable to assume that a manager is in control of the number of calls the reps make each day.
>
> How about Revenue? (After much consideration) Nope. A manager can direct some activities that might ultimately influence Revenue but can't actually direct that number to change. Though many have tried.
>
> Share of Wallet[3] with Existing Customers? Also a no. A manager can direct some activities that might ultimately influence how much of a customer's business they award to a seller, but a manager certainly can't direct the number to change—the customers have to consent.
>
> Percentage of Account Plans Completed? Yes. A manager can certainly direct his or her salespeople to complete their account plans. Again, perhaps there will be issues of compliance, but that is not the metric's fault.

And so it went, 306 times. Over and over again.

We wish we could report that this process took only a few hours, but in fact, it took days, weeks, and even months before we had sorted, unsorted, categorized, recategorized, and otherwise tortured the numbers until they confessed to their true nature. We would make a breakthrough, take a few days off to work with clients, then return to determine that we had gotten it wrong earlier in the week. Back to the whiteboard.

---

3. Share of Wallet is the amount of your customer's business that you receive relative to your competitors. If your customer fulfills its need for a certain product by purchasing half from you and half from your competitors, then you have a 50% share of that customer's wallet.

It is remarkable how difficult it can be to squeeze simplicity and order out of complexity and chaos. But day by day and iteration by iteration, each of the metrics on the wall slowly found its home in a category, and then a subcategory. Eventually, our single question led us to a framework of metrics that we believe reflects the realities of managing a sales force. Or more precisely, it reveals how a sales force *can* be managed and how a sales force can't.

ACTIVITIES, RESULTS, AND THE STUFF IN-BETWEEN

In the end, we discovered that some sales numbers *are* in fact quite manageable. These are metrics that relate to field-level activities. At the other extreme, we determined that many numbers are *completely* unmanageable. These metrics track high-level corporate results. We then teased out a third category of numbers that lies somewhere in between—not really manageable, but vulnerable to influence. These middle-ground metrics refer to the sales force's objectives that serve as a pathway from activities to results. To take you along our journey, we will examine each of the three categories in the order that they came into focus for us.

Sales Activities

Let us start with the easy one. We were pleased to discover that there are many metrics on war room walls that can truly be managed. In fact, 17% of the metrics in our study were deemed to be highly manageable. Of course, that means that more than 80% of the metrics on the walls of sales forces around the world can *not* be directly influenced by management, but we will reveal shortly that there is hope for those metrics yet.

The metrics that we found to be highly manageable are similar to the ones cited just previously—Time Spent Coaching Reps, Number of Calls Made per Day, or Number of Call Plans Completed. Basically, the 17% of the numbers on the wall that are manageable can all be associated with salesperson or sales management activities. Sample measures of what we are calling *Sales Activities* include metrics like these:

- Number of Sales Calls Made per Rep
- Percentage of Reps Using CRM
- Percentage of Account Plans Completed
- Number of Accounts Assigned per Rep
- Number of Reps Assigned per Manager
- Dollars Spent on Rep Training

Sales Activity metrics are used to quantify and track the day-to-day "doings" of the sales force. What are the sales reps doing? How are they doing it? What is the sales manager doing to enable and support them? Making phone calls, completing strategic account plans, visiting prospects, attending training events, writing proposals, coaching reps, meeting with customers—the list of potential doings goes on and on.

In a sales force, these are things that you can physically see and touch. We can't see or touch Revenue, but we can see our sales reps going on sales calls and hope that Revenue follows. We can't see or touch Share of Wallet, but we can see reps creating account plans and hope that their customers buy more from us as a consequence. Sales Activities are the causes that lead to other effects.

These sales force activities and their associated metrics are also the things that *can* be controlled by management. In fact, they are the only numbers on the war room wall that can be willed to change. The actions of our salespeople and managers will *influence* the other 80% of the metrics on the wall, but these metrics are out of our direct control. They are merely the outcomes of all our doings.

Our research therefore informed us of an irrefutable fact:

[Activities can be managed—outcomes can't.]

At a glance, this observation seems quite obvious. Of course you can only manage activities. Who needs to read a 200-page book to learn that? Well, it's a little less obvious than you might think. When we share this research with sales leaders around the country, one curious phrase is heard again and again from participants who suddenly face this reality: "It's like I just got hit in the forehead by a brick." This confession is usually followed by a short list of critical Sales Activities that they are going to begin measuring.

Apparently, a lot of smart, successful people have spent much of their careers attempting to manage things that in hindsight were obviously unmanageable. And equally as troubling, they've been neglecting to measure the things that they obviously should.

Regarding the inability to see the forest for the trees, we were as guilty as anyone else. Until The Question forced us to individually torture 306 innocent metrics, we too would have claimed the power to manage much more than we actually could. But when we very carefully examined what a sales manager can actually *do*, it came down to allocating company resources and directing the activities of their salespeople. So people can talk loosely about managing revenue or managing profit, but in the end, leaders can only manage things in their direct control. To sum it up, the Sales Activity metrics are where all the action is.

Business Results

Now we will move from the lowest level of metrics to the highest level that we found in our study. Business Results are the culmination of all that an organization does. In fact, these metrics are at such a high level that they can be influenced by factors well beyond the sales organization—finance, manufacturing, marketing, or even external troublemakers like the competition or the economy can help these numbers budge. Comprising 24% of the metrics on our wall, examples of Business Result metrics include:

- Revenue Growth
- Percentage Share of Market

- Gross Profit
- Customer Satisfaction Rating

At the highest level, Business Result metrics help us assess the overall health of our company. Are we growing or shrinking? Are we making a profit? Are we winning against the competition? Are our customers satisfied? These are the top-line numbers that everyone in the organization, including its shareholders, uses to gauge the success or failure of a business entity. These are also the metrics that go in financial statements and annual reports for the rest of the world to see. They're pretty important and very high-profile numbers.

When we compare metrics like Number of Calls Made to metrics like Revenue, it is easy to judge the dramatic disparity in the amount of control we can exert over Sales Activities versus Business Results. If our lives suddenly depended on "making the number," we would strongly prefer that the number be something actionable like Time Spent Coaching Reps, rather than Customer Satisfaction. At least our fate would be in our own highly motivated and in-control hands.

While some people will struggle to abandon the notion of "managing" Revenue, the truth is that we have virtually no direct control over Revenue or any other Business Result. Yes, there are things we can do to *influence* these outcomes—many things in fact. But we can no more command the numbers to change on our corporate report card than we can command the letters to change on the report cards of our children. All we can do is manage what is in our direct control and expect the desired outcomes to follow.

We find this concept to be both discouraging and empowering. It is somewhat discouraging because it takes from us the notion that we are in strict control of our future. We've gone through our lives largely believing that we could manage a lot of things that we ultimately can't—high-level outcomes that are influenced by many factors. However, the concept feels simultaneously empowering because it shifts our attention to the present, where we can focus on the things that we can actually control—the "doings" that we see around us every day.

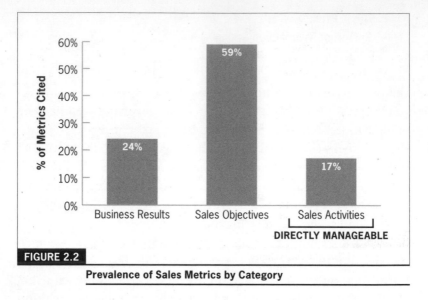

FIGURE 2.2

Prevalence of Sales Metrics by Category

Sales Objectives

Sales Activities and Business Results were not the only metrics on our wall, though. Between the extremes of action and out-come is a category of metric that serves as an intermediate step to get from one to the other. These metrics can be considered guideposts for Sales Activities to ensure that they are pointed in the right direction for the Business Results to materialize. Consequently, we labeled them *Sales Objectives*. See Figure 2.2.

As we posed The Question to our collection of metrics, Sales Objectives were the most vexing of them all. They were so susceptible to influence that we felt like sales management *should* be able to manage them if it put forth the right effort, but the objectives clearly were not activities that could be seen or touched like making phone calls or completing account plans. Most of them had no inherent organizational value like Revenue or Market Share; in fact, many parts of an organization would not care about the metrics at all.

These metrics are really unique goals for the sales force. They are Sales Objectives that are either given to sales manage-ment from above or identified by the sales force itself. Within

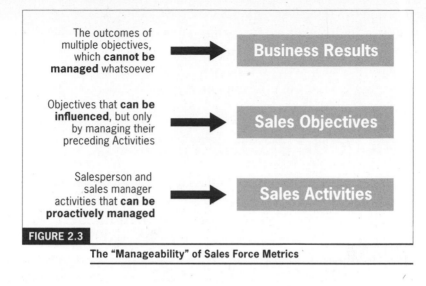

FIGURE 2.3

The "Manageability" of Sales Force Metrics

the 59% of our metrics that fell into this category, we observed measures such as these:

- Percentage Share of Wallet
- Number of New Customers Acquired
- Days Ramp-Up Time for New Salespeople
- Percentage Customer Retention
- Percentage of Target Customers Contacted

It's easy to see how many of these metrics feel as though they are within our control. I should be able to increase my Share of Wallet with existing customers if I just do more thoughtful account planning. And I should be able to acquire more new customers if I just do more prospecting. And I should be able to shorten the ramp-up time for new salespeople if I just do more training. Every time we asked these metrics, "Hey, can I manage you?" the answer was always, "Sure, if I just do . . ." Figure 2.3 summarizes our findings.

These metrics are not highly manageable, but they can be directly influenced by pointing certain Sales Activities at them. Again and again, we had the same conversation with these metrics: "Hey, can we manage *<insert Sales Objective>*? Well, probably so, if we just *<insert Sales Activity>*." While it was initially quite difficult to distinguish these two types of metrics from one another, we soon found that the nature of our struggle to separate Sales Activities and Sales Objectives was our first big stride toward cracking the sales management code.

THE CODE BEGINS TO CRACK

To have control over something, it is fundamental that we understand the cause-and-effect relationship between the action we take and the outcome we expect. If we press the accelerator on the floor of our car, we expect the car to go faster. If we turn the steering wheel to the left, we expect the car to follow. Sales management has long been standing on the accelerator, and it periodically needs to turn the wheel as well. However, our sales forces do not respond with the same predictability as an automobile because sales management has not had a thorough knowledge of the cause-and-effect relationships at work in its organizations.

This is why our struggle to separate Sales Activities from Sales Objectives was so critical. It became apparent that there is a very tight causal relationship between these two layers of metrics. All other things being equal, managing certain Sales Activities leads directly to the achievement of certain Sales Objectives. If you want more new customers, do more prospecting. If you want greater Share of Wallet, do more account planning. If you want new salespeople to reach full productivity sooner, do more training. Once the pattern emerged, we became quite skilled matchmakers between the two layers of metrics.

Like discovering that we can only manage activities, discovering that we can fairly predictably achieve certain Sales Objectives by managing specific Sales Activities also has an element of "duh" to it. *Of course* that's how we achieve our objectives—by doing the right things to get us there. However, we have seen more brick strikes than "duh" responses when we share these insights with sales leaders. Let us explain why this is the case.

It turns out that management is quite good at telling sales-people what it wants (the Sales Objectives). However, managers aren't always as diligent in providing sales reps with explicit guidance on how they should do it (the Sales Activities). How many sales managers tell their reps that they need to get more sales from existing accounts? Many more than actually sit down with their reps and help them do focused account planning. How many managers tell their salespeople to go get new customers? Many more than take the time to help their reps map out a focused prospecting strategy.

The flying brick here is not that doing specific things will lead to certain outcomes. The insight is that *if you want certain outcomes, you have to do specific things*. If you want higher Share of Wallet, your salespeople have to do good account planning. If you want more new customers, your reps have to develop detailed plans for effective prospecting. Asking for specific Sales Objectives without ensuring that the proper Sales Activities are in place is not necessarily a recipe for inevitable disaster, but it is certainly a recipe for unpredictable and (more importantly) uncontrollable performance.

We found a similar relationship between the two higher levels of metrics—Sales Objectives and Business Results. We observed that certain Business Results can be achieved by pointing certain Sales Objectives at them. For example, if your company desires greater Market Share, one path would be to set a Sales Objective of attaining a greater Share of Wallet within your existing customers. Or if your company desires more Revenue, one path would be to set a Sales Objective of acquiring new customers. Again, the value in this observation is not that achieving specific objectives yields desired results. The insight is that *to yield desired results, you must set specific objectives* (see Figure 2.4).

This seems a reasonable expectation—for leadership to not only ask for a Business Result such as increased Market Share but to also identify the Sales Objective like greater Share of Wallet that they want the sales force to pursue in order to achieve it. Yet, how many sales forces are given little more direction than to hit a revenue target? And how many sales reps

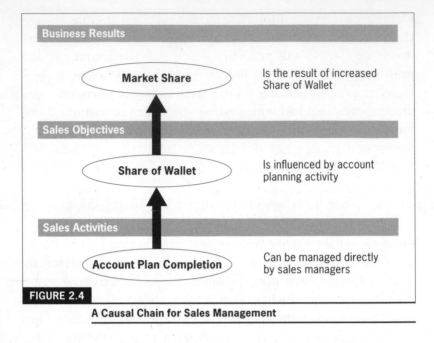

FIGURE 2.4

A Causal Chain for Sales Management

receive little more guidance than to make their little sliver of that overall revenue number? Millions.

If no more direction is given to the field than to achieve a Business Result, then management has only itself to blame when it cannot exert control over its sales force's performance. Sales managers and reps are then left to chart their own paths to the top of the metrics hierarchy, and it is certain that they will do it in as many different ways as there are people in the sales force. Most troubling, they will do it with little visibility into their plans and as little accountability for their actions.

The sales management code starts to crack when leadership provides its sales force with a clear path from the bottom to the top. It cracks when everyone in the field understands what they must do at the Sales Activity level to achieve specific Sales Objectives and the consequent Business Results. If the expectation is set that Market Share must increase, then the explicit expectations should also be set that this will be accomplished through greater Share of Wallet driven by increased account planning activities by salespeople. *And* target metrics should be identified and tracked for all three of those expectations. When the war room wall reveals that Market Share is not increasing as desired, it will probably also reveal the sources of the problem, lagging Share of Wallet driven by insufficient or ineffective account planning. *Then* management can provide clear directives to the field with confidence that they will move the numbers on the wall.

STATUS CHECK

We identified three discrete levels of sales force metrics.

1. **Sales Activities**, which are highly manageable and whose associated metrics can be moved at will
2. **Sales Objectives**, which can be directly influenced and whose associated metrics can be driven by managing certain Sales Activities
3. **Business Results**, which are wholly unmanageable but whose associated metrics are determined by the achievement of specific Sales Objectives

Even more important, we established causal relationships among the three levels. Sales Activities drive Sales Objectives, which in turn drive Business Results. For example, if you do more account planning, you can achieve greater Share of Wallet, which should in turn lead to greater Market Share.

Understanding how the causal relationships work up the chain is not as important, though, as the ability to reverse-engineer the relationships. If a corporate goal for the year is to increase your Revenue, then you need to choose a specific Sales Objective that will most likely lead to the achievement of that Business Result. If you determine that increasing your Number of New Customers is the best available path, you know you must manage the Sales Activities that will strongly influence that metric—in this case, increased prospecting.

Of course, you should also associate relevant metrics with each of these levels in order to track compliance with the activities and to

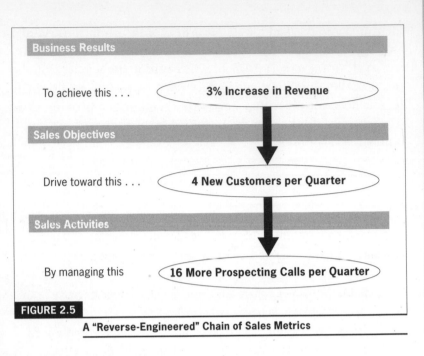

FIGURE 2.5

A "Reverse-Engineered" Chain of Sales Metrics

measure progress toward the Objective and Result. Say that your target increase in Revenue is 3%. You might determine through analysis that each rep needs to recruit four new customers per quarter to achieve this Business Result. You might then calculate that each rep needs to make 16 additional prospecting calls per quarter to predictably expect to win four new customers. As a sales manager, you can now set explicit expectations with your reps down to the level of Sales Activity. Your reps will know what to do. You will know what to manage. You will now be able to confidently exert control over your sales force's performance. See Figure 2.5.

At this point in our journey, we had uncovered some very important insights into the challenges and limitations of sales management:

- We discovered that not all sales metrics are on par with one another. Some of the numbers on war room walls *can* be managed with the degree of control that leadership expects, but more than 80% of those numbers can only be influenced *indirectly*.

- We established a series of causal relationships that can be used to coerce those unmanageable numbers with a high degree of certainty. Managing Sales Activities leads to the achievement of Sales Objectives, which in turn leads to the attainment of Business Results.
- We identified a means to reverse-engineer high-level corporate goals and connect them to sales force activities. Beginning with the end in mind allows us to architect a series of interrelated metrics that enable us to manage toward our desired outcomes.

Looking back at our point of departure, we felt like we had written the first few pages of the desperately needed operating instructions for a sales force. The numbers on the wall now had more meaning, and we'd learned a bit about how they can be used to exert control over sales force performance. However, we didn't feel that we had cracked the code. We needed to learn more about how the numbers actually work.

Business Results— the Company's Health

CHAPTER 3

BACK TO THE WAR ROOM

The fiscal year just ended, and the war room is rockin'.

Excitement is in the air, as the entire leadership team awaits its first glimpse of the company's year-end numbers. Conversations swirl about the year's big victories over the competition. People are thankful for the last-minute deals that closed just in time to be booked in Q4. Twelve long months of hard work have led to this single moment in time. All eyes are on the walls as the numbers begin to post.

So which numbers will be the stars of today's party? The Number of Sales Calls that the sales force was able to make last year? That would be useful information if management were here to direct Sales Activities, but that is not today's purpose. How about the Number of New Customers that were acquired during the year? That will be interesting to explore later, but even Sales Objectives are not important today.

The numbers that will make or break the mood in this war room are all Business Results. Did the company hit its Revenue target for the year? Did it eke out enough Profit to satisfy investors? These are the numbers that everyone has gathered here to see. Not measures of Sales Activities or Sales Objectives—just Revenue and Profit. Is this intense focus on Business Results short-sighted by senior management? No, it is not. In fact, this is how it should be.

Make no mistake—Business Results are the most important numbers on the wall. They are the corporate endgame. This is because Business Results are the primary measures of a company's overall health. These metrics include such key performance indicators as Revenue, Profit, Market Share, and Customer Satisfaction—things that eventually find their way into financial statements and annual reports. These few measurements afford even casual observers a crystal-clear snapshot of an organization's well-being. Good numbers reveal a healthy company. Bad numbers? Well, let's not even think about that.

This is the primary function of Business Results—to gauge the general condition of a corporate entity. Far removed from any specific action of any individual, these measures are the culmination of the collective effort of an entire enterprise. Marketing, manufacturing, sales, and executive leadership, among others, all contribute to growth in revenue or increases in market share. When Business Results trend upward, everyone in the organization will take credit. When they trend downward, everyone will credibly point in the other direction. Unlike Sales Objectives or Sales Activities, any part of a company can lay claim to or disavow themselves of the outcomes that are Business Results. They are simply measures of overall corporate health.

DOING WELL

In our personal lives, this is the type of information we want when we ask about an old friend, "How is he doing these days?" What we hope to hear in response is, "He's doing great! He likes his job, is in great health, has lots of friends, a good family. Overall, he's doing well." Business Results measure the corporate equivalent of "well." If the company is growing, generates lots of cash, has a good position in the marketplace, and is loved

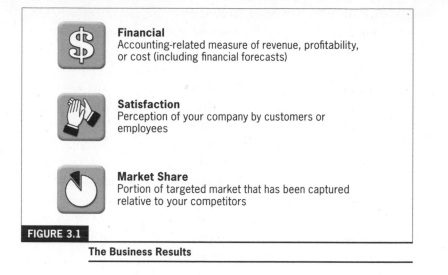

Financial
Accounting-related measure of revenue, profitability, or cost (including financial forecasts)

Satisfaction
Perception of your company by customers or employees

Market Share
Portion of targeted market that has been captured relative to your competitors

FIGURE 3.1

The Business Results

by its customers, overall, it's doing very well. See Figure 3.1 for the three main measures of Business Results.

As you might imagine, we found several different ways to measure a company's well-being. First, there are metrics used for self-examination that we called *Financial*. These are measures of health that the company defines for itself. How much Revenue does it want? How much Profitability would be considered a good Return on Investment? These Business Results are the objective financial parameters that leadership uses to judge its own progress toward its self-defined standards for "doing well."

Second is a set of measurements that reflects the perceptions of others. They reveal how healthy the company appears to others whose opinions it values. We chose to label these measures *Satisfaction*, and they include the opinions of both an organization's customers and its employees. Distinct from self-imposed Financial metrics, these numbers are highly subjective, and the criteria are largely defined by the customers' and employees' own personal experiences. See Figure 3.2.

Finally, we found a category of metrics that evaluates a company's health relative to its peers. Measures of *Market Share* put success in the context of a competitive environment and assess

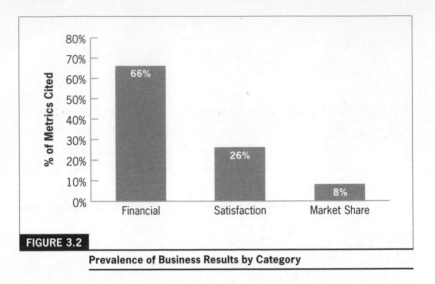

FIGURE 3.2

Prevalence of Business Results by Category

which company has the healthier organization. In some industries, Market Share is the primary indicator of well-being, and a shrinking share of the market can spell certain death.

In sum, we identified categories of performance metrics that examine a company's health from several perspectives:

- Do *we* think our company is healthy?
- Do *others* think it is healthy?
- Is it healthy *compared to its peers*?

All good questions. Now let's take a deeper look at what the answers might be for each.

It's All About the Financials

In the history of sales management, there is unquestionably an alpha metric—the very first measure by which a sales force was ever judged: Revenue. Even today, it is an obsession for almost every organization with which we work. Public companies are measured by it, CEOs' egos are fueled by it, chief sales officers are fired because of it, field salespeople are motivated by it, and incentive compensation is driven by it. Ah, sweet Revenue, the all-powerful performance metric that needs no introduction.

The other Financial metrics we encountered in our research also command considerable reverence. Long before there were the concepts of Customer Satisfaction, Market Share, or a Sales Pipeline, there were these fundamental accounting entries that eventually determine the life or death of every company. Go too long with low Revenue and no Profits, and the company doors are shuttered. As measures of corporate health go, these are the few vital signs that cannot be ignored. If these measures turn bad, nothing else can save you—it's off to the crowded graveyard of failed businesses.

It is no surprise, then, that Financial metrics are the most predominant Business Results in our study. (See Figure 3.6.) They are the biggest and boldest numbers on War Room walls around the globe, and everyone in a company should have at least some interest in what they have to say. This is especially true of senior leadership, which is ultimately accountable for the story that the numbers tell.

As we wrote earlier, these numbers represent leadership's own definition of a healthy company. Reporting $500 million in revenue and $100 million in profits doesn't really tell a story unless the numbers are put into the context of a specific organization's expectations. For GE or Wal-Mart, these numbers would communicate the equivalent of extinction. But for most small businesses, these numbers would tell a story of wild success. Unless the numbers spin a tale so tragic that it leads to bankruptcy, leadership itself is responsible for setting healthy expectations for its organization and the organization's stakeholders.

Really, Financial metrics require little explanation. Managers have been collecting and reporting these numbers for centuries, so we will not force you to endure our redefining the obvious. However, there is one characteristic of Financial metrics that is worth exploring because it caused us considerable angst as we shuffled the metrics around on our war room wall.

Financial metrics, and Revenue numbers in particular, were frustratingly meddlesome as we stared at the wall trying to put the numbers into our crisp, clean categories of Results, Objectives, and Activities. This is because of the uncontrollable need by management to assign a Financial number to everything in its organization. Since these metrics are easily allocated using basic managerial accounting principles, almost everything in a company is likely to have a Revenue or Profit allocation assigned to it. What we found, then, were very confusing, multilayer measures that we came to call *compound metrics*.

When we saw a metric like Percentage Revenue Growth, we knew exactly what to do with it—into the Financial metrics bucket it went. However, when we encountered a measure like Revenue per Product Type, we were initially frozen in our tracks. Should that go into the Financial bucket since it's a measure of Revenue, or should it count as a Sales Objective since it is tracking success in selling particular products?

Or if we came across Revenue per Sales Call, is that a Business Result since it is quantified in dollars, or should we categorize it as a Sales Activity metric since it refers to the activity of reps making sales calls?

It quickly became apparent that Revenue can be assigned to almost anything you can imagine. We eventually concluded that these compound metrics were best thought of as basic fractions with a numerator and a denominator. For sales management, Revenue seemed to be the numerator of choice where Anything was the denominator. Over and over again, we encountered this frequently cited metric: *Revenue per Anything*.

Revenue per Rep, Revenue per Product Type, Revenue per Existing Account, Revenue per Stage of Sales Cycle—the New Question that had us baffled was this:

> **What did "Revenue per Anything" really measure—the Revenue or the Anything?**

This was a critical learning point for us as we tortured both ourselves and the numbers. After a good deal of ruminating, we concluded that the *metric* itself is not as important as *what it is intended to measure* (see Figure 3.3). With "simple" measures, such as Revenue Growth or Profitability, it was pretty clear that

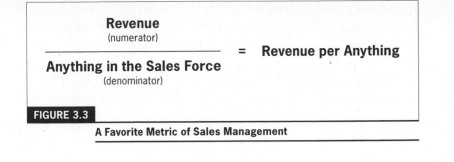

$$\frac{\text{Revenue (numerator)}}{\text{Anything in the Sales Force (denominator)}} = \text{Revenue per Anything}$$

FIGURE 3.3

A Favorite Metric of Sales Management

these metrics belong in the Business Results category. They were almost certainly intended to gauge the overall health of the company. The question this metric answers is whether the company is achieving its endgame goals that it set for itself.

With the more complex compound metrics, we decided that they are most likely intended to measure the denominator of Anything rather than the numerator of Revenue. For instance, Revenue Growth from New Products is probably not intended as a yardstick for Revenue Growth—otherwise you could just measure Revenue Growth. It's most likely used to gauge success in selling New Products, so it therefore belongs in the Sales Objective category. The objective is to sell more new products, and an easy way to measure progress toward that is to report whether revenue from new products is actually growing. Makes sense.

This phenomenon of designing elaborate metrics can be taken to extremes, and some of our more sophisticated clients like to push the boundaries. Take for instance a measure like Revenue from New Products by Stage of the Sales Cycle per Rep. Upon examination, this is not intended to measure Revenue, nor New Product sales, nor the Sales Cycle, though it might appear so at first glance (and second glance, and third). In reality, it is meant to measure the effectiveness of the Rep in selling new products, as measured by moving associated Revenue through the Sales Cycle (see Figure 3.4). Deciphering sales metrics can be quite an exhausting exercise.

Of course, other Financial metrics can be equally as tiring, since we can assign Profits to just as many Anythings as we can

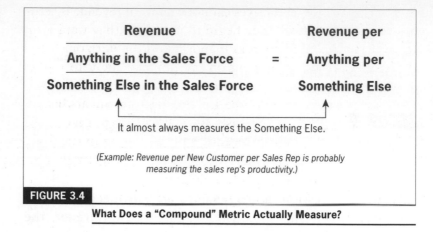

FIGURE 3.4

What Does a "Compound" Metric Actually Measure?

assign Revenue. Regardless of the compound metric, it almost always ends up as an actual measure of the denominator—Anything. As we learned to look for the denominators on our wall, the sales management code began to crack a little more easily.

Again, the most important takeaway from our examination of Financial metrics is the realization that we could not categorize a metric solely by the terms in its description. To accurately understand the value of a sales measurement, we must first determine what the number is actually intended to measure. These seemingly subtle distinctions will become quite important when we eventually get to the business of architecting a coherent and aligned system of sales force metrics.

The Case of the Disappearing Sales Pipeline

As we mentioned earlier in this chapter, Financial metrics (and in particular Revenue) are the lifeblood of any company. If ample revenue is not coming in the door to squeeze out some profit, then the door will eventually slam shut. And if the revenue coming in is sufficient to keep it open but *insufficient* to meet the company's expectations, then that very same door becomes an exit for the company's senior executives.

For that reason, executives cannot wait until revenue is actually *in* the door before they begin to watch it—they want it on the war room wall as soon as it appears on the horizon. It has therefore become incumbent on sales management to report *anticipated* revenue from in-process sales opportunities. They do so in an assortment of hypothetical financial statements known collectively as *forecasts*. Forecasts allow executives to gaze in the future, predict how much revenue will be coming in the door, and manage their stakeholders' expectations appropriately. This keeps the doors open, but only as an entrance.

Without question, management's *favorite* mechanism for real-time forecasting is the sales pipeline.[1] Like Revenue, the sales pipeline really needs no introduction—every war room wall has some pipeline numbers on it. Appropriately, our study contained a good portion of metrics that were used to report the size, shape, and complexion of a sales pipeline. They included measures like these:

- Total Pipeline Revenue
- Number of Deals in Each Stage of the Sales Cycle
- Percentage of Deals Advancing by Stage
- Days Length of Sales Cycle

As we began to receive these metrics from our surveyed companies, we dutifully created a space on our wall for "Sales Pipeline" metrics. This category, we thought, was going to be the easiest of them all—if a metric had the term *pipeline* or *sales cycle* in it, then just throw it in the "Sales Pipeline" bucket. And conveniently, almost every company had already designated a category of pipeline metrics on its own, so it was a simple task for us to shuffle them to our sales pipeline space. But as we stared at these metrics over time, the pipeline numbers came to befuddle us.

Initially, we had the sales pipeline metrics in the "totally unmanageable" category that later became Business Results. This made sense because most all of the metrics in this category

---

1. Also referred to as a *sales funnel*.

were quantified in dollars—*Dollars* in the Sales Pipeline, *Dollars* in Each Stage of the Sales Cycle, and so on. Of course, these dollars would eventually turn into Revenue, and we had already established that Revenue could not be managed. So sales pipeline metrics must be Business Results. Not manageable.

But once we created Sales Objectives as our third level of "influenceable" metrics, our eyes kept darting back and forth between those and our "Sales Pipeline" metrics like Percentage of Deals Won or Percentage of Deals Advancing. It would seem that a sales manager *should* be able to influence these metrics by coaching and developing her reps into more skilled sellers. In fact, if the sales manager could *not* influence metrics such as Percentage of Deals Won, then you'd have to fundamentally question the value of even having sales managers. Managers had better be able to influence the sales pipeline, or else their sales forces are in trouble.

Our suspicion that the "Sales Pipeline" category was too diverse kept nagging us, but objects at rest tend to stay at rest. Without any better way to characterize them, the Sales Pipeline metrics remained right where they were on our wall, as unmanageable Business Results.

They remained there until we had the epiphany that we discussed earlier: the metric itself is not as important as *what* it is intended to measure. We had fallen into the trap of letting the label on the metric define it for us. We needed to examine the *nature* of the metric to discover where it belonged on the wall. Finally, we had a new question that would help overcome the inertia of the Sales Pipeline metrics. So we began to interrogate the pipeline numbers with our new question, What are you really intending to measure?

It became quickly apparent that sales pipeline metrics have two distinct uses. The first intended use is to measure the health of the company looking into the future. These are metrics such as Total Pipeline Revenue or Weighted Value of the Pipeline, and they are typically reported at the corporate level. By assigning dollar amounts and probabilities to various milestones in its sales force's aggregated opportunities, management can build a credible sales forecast for its overall organization. And this is

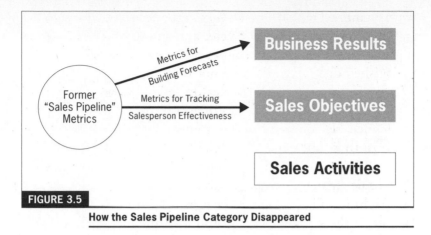

FIGURE 3.5

How the Sales Pipeline Category Disappeared

the primary objective of these pipeline metrics on the war room walls—to create a probability-weighted financial statement that foretells good or bad future Business Results.

The second use of sales pipeline metrics is to measure the effectiveness of salespeople at moving opportunities through their sales cycles. These are measurements like Percentage of Deals Advancing or Percentage of Deals Won, and they are typically reported at the individual level. They are not intended to create financial statements like their corporate-level peers but rather are used by sales management as diagnostic and objective-setting tools to improve salesperson productivity. By identifying where a seller's deals are getting stuck in the sales cycle, a manager can provide guidance or support to help the salesperson move further down the path to success.[2]

We therefore began to pull metrics out of the Sales Pipeline bucket and put them into one of two places (see Figure 3.5). Any metric that looked as though it was intended to measure the future health of the company remained at the Business Result level, but it was reallocated to the bucket of Financial

---

2. Note that measures that average financial outcomes across an entire company's population (such as Average Sales per Employee) remained at the Business Result level, because they are typically used to benchmark overall company productivity. Metrics were only moved to the Sales Objective level if they were reported for individual sellers, which measures salesperson capability.

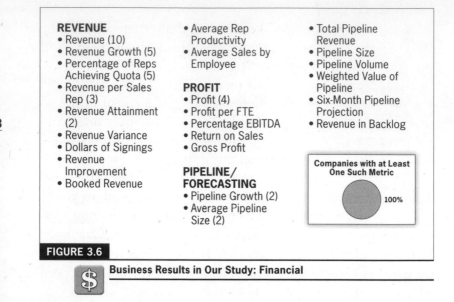

FIGURE 3.6

Business Results in Our Study: Financial

measures where numbers like Revenue already lived. Whether it is booked Revenue or forecasted Revenue, the metrics both answer the same basic question: is this company healthy?

Any metric that was intended to measure the effectiveness of a seller at shepherding deals through his pipeline was moved to the Sales Objective level. Sales managers could then influence these measures through Sales Activities like coaching and training. We then breathed a sigh of relief, knowing that our management framework now allowed for sales managers to sway things like Percentage of Deals Won. But most important, our model now more closely resembled the reality that we knew.

So our breakthrough with the sales pipeline metrics was to separate the "forecasting" measures from the "salesperson effectiveness" measures. The forecasting metrics went into the Financial bucket within Business Results, and the effectiveness metrics went into a to-be-determined bucket within Sales Objectives. Our nagging concerns about the pipeline metrics had disappeared, but so had our "Sales Pipeline" category. We now had only three buckets within Business Results—Financial, Satisfaction, and Market Share. Life was much simpler. See Figure 3.6.

Satisfied Yet?

As much as people like to think about themselves, they *love* to know what other people think about them. And though most individuals don't go around routinely surveying their colleagues to assess their own likability, companies have a seemingly insatiable appetite for exactly that type of information. To a corporate entity, "likability" is commonly measured as "Satisfaction," and we found that 26% of our Business Results metrics were some variation on this theme.

Measures of Satisfaction are a different kind of health-check. They are the equivalent of "How healthy do I look to you?" There are two primary audiences for these cosmetic inquiries, both the company's customers and its employees. Customer Satisfaction metrics constitute most of the Satisfaction numbers we saw, and they were quantified through measures like these:

- Overall Customer Satisfaction
- Ease-of-Doing-Business Index
- Percentage of Customers with Intent to Refer

Leadership also cares greatly about the perceptions of its employees, and our research reflects this fact. In our data were employee-facing measurements like:

- Employee Satisfaction Index
- Employee Intent to Stay
- Employee Engagement Index

Both categories of Satisfaction metrics shared a couple of similar qualities. First, they were both mostly calculated using indexes, rather than the units of percentages, dollars, or hours that quantify most other sales metrics. This is because satisfaction is a subjective and nonstandard measure that must be force-fit into a contrived scale, typically between one and five, that measures from "totally unsatisfied" to "totally satisfied." We have seen companies actually attempt to convert Satisfaction measures into associated dollar amounts, but their success with the endeavor was questionable, at best.

The second similarity between the Customer Satisfaction and Employee Satisfaction metrics is that in both cases leadership collected both generalized and more focused measures of satisfaction. Two questions that exemplify the distinction would be "How satisfied are you with our company?" versus "How satisfied are you as a user of our CRM tool?" The second question is somewhat more tactical and could be more useful, depending on the company's purpose for gathering the data. As a rule, the more specific a Satisfaction measure gets, the more practical it becomes as a management tool.

Like most of the numbers on our wall, Satisfaction metrics challenged us to find their rightful place in our management framework. The nature of their challenge was to identify whether satisfaction is a Sales Objective or a Business Result. At first we thought that measures of Satisfaction fit perfectly as Sales Objectives. If the sales force can do specific things to make customers more satisfied, then certainly that would drive increased sales and consequently increased revenue for the organization.

However, study after study has shown that the causal link between Customer Satisfaction and actual purchasing behavior is highly suspect.[3] In the real world, customers might be quite satisfied with your products and your company, yet they can be lured away to a competitor for any number of reasons beyond your control. A colleague might convince them that your competitor has a better product, a superior may force them to switch allegiances, or a competitor's salesperson might simply catch them in a moment of weakness. Regardless, Customer Satisfaction has not been definitively shown to drive purchasing behavior, so therefore it cannot credibly be considered a Sales Objective in our model.

Similarly, the direct impact of Employee Satisfaction on financial performance is annoyingly uncertain. Most research we have read confirms a *correlation* between Employee

---

3. One of the most influential studies on Customer Satisfaction metrics and their tenuous link to profitability, "The One Number You Need to Grow" by Frederick F. Reichheld, was published in the *Harvard Business Review* in December 2003.

Satisfaction and organizational success, but it remains unproven whether happier employees cause a company to succeed or if a successful work environment makes for happier employees. Chicken → Egg → Chicken? Successful → Satisfied → Successful? We may never know.

Regardless, both Customer Satisfaction and Employee Satisfaction are unquestionably indicative of a company's health. Whether or not happier customers and happier salespeople will improve financial performance is unclear, but unhappy customers and miserable salespeople simply cannot be a good thing. Therefore, we felt comfortable categorizing Satisfaction as a Business Result—a key indicator of company health, and something that must be purposefully influenced through the management of certain Sales Activities and their related Objectives.

We have a bit of a love-hate relationship with satisfaction surveys. On the love side, we view them as useful vehicles to collect candid feedback that might otherwise go unheard by management. One might expect the sales force to be an effective communication channel for customer feedback, but salespeople can actually serve as an unintentional filter for valuable customer insights. Ironically, we find that salespeople are often blind to burning customer issues—even when the blaze is plainly visible to others.

There is a "Curse of Intimacy" that sometimes settles on a sales force that enjoys long-term relationships with its customers. After years of repeated interactions, salespeople can become numb to subtle signals from their customers that would be completely apparent to a bystander. Further, intimacy can breed the false assumption that customers will openly reveal all of their concerns to their salesperson. Sellers will often say, "I don't need to constantly ask that customer how we're doing. I've known him for 20 years, and I talk to him every week. If he has a problem with us, he'll let me know." Maybe.

To provide a possibly familiar example of being ambushed by the Curse of Intimacy, I had a friend many years ago whose girlfriend brought their relationship to an abrupt end. Totally unexpectedly, she announced that she was terminating the friendship—immediately. After the obvious interrogation, it became apparent that there were no other contributing factors. She simply was unhappy in the relationship and had decided that it was time to get out.

By his account her actions "came out of nowhere," and yet, though I am not the most perceptive person in the world, it was pretty obvious to me that their relationship had been going downhill for a while. In fairness to my friend, it *is* hard to notice stuff like that when you're too close to the action, and that is exactly where most salespeople find themselves with their very best customers—extremely close to the action. While maintaining clear communications with your best customers is absolutely critical, intimacy can actually inhibit the flow of meaningful information and deaden a seller's awareness to otherwise apparent signs of trouble.

From this perspective, satisfaction surveys are intuitively appealing. They give customers, or in some cases employees, the opportunity to provide candid feedback in a sterile, non-threatening environment. Surveys are also relatively low-cost, so they enable data collection on a scale that is useful for analysis. They therefore *can be* a safe and productive path around the Curse of Intimacy. But there is one big pothole on that path that counterbalances our love-hate quotient.

A little data is a dangerous thing. Though one might tend to believe that *any* data is good data, gathering insufficient or inaccurate data is far worse than gathering no data at all. A theme of this book is that when good metrics are used properly, they provide managers with the insights to make good decisions and the ability to drive change. Conversely, inadequate or misinterpreted data can cause the wrong decisions to be made, which can have a devastating effect when the wrong kind of change is implemented.

Most satisfaction surveys fall into the territory of inadequate information from a management perspective. This is because they provide only an averaged index number that has no objective value and little direct relationship to the practical world. If your company makes $100 million in profit, you know exactly what that means: your company now has 100 million more

CUSTOMER
- Customer Satisfaction (4)
- Customer Satisfaction Index
- Customer Satisfaction Ratings
- Number of Customer Referrals
- Percentage Customers Satisfied
- Percentage of Customers with Intent to Refer

- Customer Loyalty Index
- Satisfaction Rates
- Ease of Doing Business Index

EMPLOYEE
- Employee Satisfaction Index
- Sales Force Engagement Index
- Employee Intent to Stay

- Employee Intent to Refer
- Employee Empowerment Index
- Teammate Satisfaction
- CRM Satisfaction Index

Companies with at Least One Such Metric

42%

FIGURE 3.7

Business Result Metrics in Our Study: Satisfaction

dollars in the bank than it did last year. And if you want to make $50 million more in profit next year, you know exactly what you have to do—increase your revenues or decrease your costs.

But if your customers are 4.6 satisfied, what does that mean? And if you want to raise their Customer Satisfaction to 4.9, how would you do that? This is why we refer to satisfaction indexes as applause-o-meters. Hearing your customers clap for you feels pretty good, but you can't be sure that it's loud enough, since there's no objective comparison for applause. And you'll always want to move the needle higher, but it's hard to know what compels each person to clap. Are your customers all clapping in unison, or does each have her own reasons for being satisfied? It's hard to know from a single, averaged, indexed number. Satisfaction indexes can be a lot of fun to watch, but they're difficult to understand.

So Satisfaction metrics can be useful as directional indicators of a company's health. Figure 3.7 shows the many forms these metrics take. They also allow management to leapfrog organizational information filters and gather candid feedback from its customers and employees. However, measures of Satisfaction must be kept in perspective. Like other Business Results, they are driven by many other things in an organization, and you must take care to decipher their meaning before making any management decisions. But unlike other Business Results, Satisfaction metrics are difficult to interpret because they are artificial constructs with ambiguous units of measure. So feel free to enjoy the applause, but get to know your audience to make certain you understand why they clap. Or why they boo.

Dare to Share

The final category of Business Results that we found in our research is Market Share. Almost always expressed as a percentage, this number is the portion of the total address-able market for your products or services that you have captured relative to your competitors. It is Share of Wallet on the grand-est scale—all of the wallets. This is an age-old marketing metric that can seem a bit sleepy, but we have actually seen some interesting dynamics surrounding this measurement.

In some industries like consumer products or certain industrial materials, this metric is nearly on par with Financial metrics, since the two categories are so tightly intertwined. We have worked with clients that saw Market Share as so important to their profitability that it was included in their salespeople's incentive compensation plans. In some cases, gaining significant market share even trumps profitability, as we witnessed in the dot-com boom when companies were trying to establish a "first mover advantage" at any cost. Capture enough Market Share, and the riches might eventually follow.

We have also worked with clients whose overarching goal was to keep Market Share as steady as possible. These are typically mature industries in which the competitors have settled into comfortable market positions and don't want to rock the boat. Like two dogs that previously met in a park and wrestled to establish dominance, their major battles have largely been fought, and it is desirable to avoid additional skirmishes. If one company begins to gain meaningful Market Share, a price war could ensue that would damage the entire industry's profitability. Status quo is the way to go.

And finally, we have worked with companies for which getting Market Share numbers from the leadership team was more difficult than getting their Social Security numbers and mothers' maiden names. These companies have market share so large that they effectively rule their industries. In these rare situations, advertising their dominance could draw unwanted attention from various entities that could threaten their market positions. We've known other companies that don't fear external interference, but they want their employees to behave as if they are scrappy start-ups, despite their substantial market heft. In cases such as these, success is quietly celebrated and loudly ignored.

One way in which we have seen companies struggle with Market Share is in calculating their total "addressable" market. Market Share numbers can be greatly influenced by how widely you cast your net. For example, if you are a $250 million player in a $1 billion industry, then your Market Share is nominally 25%. However, if you decide that $500 million of the industry is captive to a competitor and does not represent any real opportunity for your company's products, you might decide that only $500 million of that market is "addressable." Consequently, you could calculate your share as $250 million of a $500 million market, or 50%.

Math such as this might seem like an academic exercise, but many companies use these kinds of assumptions to size and deploy their sales forces. Taking the example we just used, you could potentially need only half as many salespeople to cover the marketplace if you decided to concede $500 million of it to your competitor. Or you might need to double the size of your sales force if you determine that the addressable market is actually $2 billion. So you can see how resource allocation and other critical management decisions can be affected by determining what your addressable market truly is.

Regardless, Market Share is a key measure of a company's health in many industries. Though it might appear exceedingly unpopular with only 8% of our Business Result metrics falling into this category, we can assure you that a higher percentage of companies are tracking Market Share data. In fact, marketing departments in most companies will have this number on the tips of their tongues, but our study only incorporated sales force

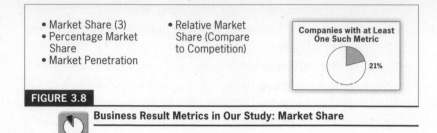

- Market Share (3)
- Percentage Market Share
- Market Penetration

- Relative Market Share (Compare to Competition)

Companies with at Least One Such Metric

21%

FIGURE 3.8

Business Result Metrics in Our Study: Market Share

metrics. At the highest level of many organizations, corporate health is all relative. See Figure 3.8.

THE PROBLEM WITH "MANAGING BY RESULTS"

Though Business Results clearly are not manageable by any direct means, this does not keep sales managers from trying. Week after week across the globe, sales managers meet with their sales forces to review their salespeople's "numbers" and to provide the sellers with counsel on how to improve them. It would be impossible to estimate how many times we've heard variations of this conversation between a sales manager and a rep:

Manager: *So let's take a look at how you're doing year-to-date with your numbers.*

(Manager and rep stare at a pipeline report, which is the agenda for their discussion.)

Rep: *Unfortunately, you can see that I'm falling behind in my Revenue numbers. I don't know if I'll be able to make my $1 million target for this quarter, and that's going to put me even further behind for the year.*

Manager: *Yes, I see that. How are you going to get that Revenue number back in line?*

Rep: *Well, I have a pretty big pipeline of business that I'm working right now.*

Manager: *Good. How big is your sales pipeline?*

Rep: *I have about $4 million in there that could potentially close by the end of the year.*

Manager: *But you'd have to win more than 50% of that to make up the ground that you've lost so far this year. That would be a pretty high win rate by historical standards.*

Rep: *Yeah, I guess you're right about that.*

Manager: *Your pipeline needs to be bigger. It should probably be more like $6 million, if you're realistically going to hit your quota.*

Rep: *Yes, that would make sense.*

Manager: *Do you think you can pump up your pipeline over the next few weeks?*

Rep: *I think so. I'll just have to work a little harder at it.*

Manager: *You can do it. Get that pipeline number up, and you'll get to your quota. I believe in you.*

Rep: *Thanks. I'll hope to have better news by the end of the month.*

Manager: *Great. Good luck.*

What you have just witnessed is "managing by results." Revenue and the size of a pipeline are both Business Results and cannot be directly managed. This conversation is the business equivalent of your doctor saying to you, "You're not looking too healthy. You'd better go get more health, or else you're not going to be healthy the next time I see you."

It's not a productive management practice to examine a Business Result and then direct the salesperson to go change the Business Result. A more productive conversation would help sales reps select the Sales Objectives that will steer them in the right direction and then set expectations for the Sales Activities that will lead them there.

That same conversation would have been more helpful if it had ended something like this:

Manager: *Your pipeline needs to be bigger. It should probably be more like $6 million if you're realistically going to hit your quota.*

Rep: *Yes, that would make sense.*

Manager: *So what are some options for increasing the size of your pipeline?*

Rep: *Well, there are only a couple of options. I could either get more opportunities in my pipeline, or I could find bigger deals [two examples of Sales Objectives].*

Manager: *I agree. Which of those objectives seems the more achievable of the two?*

Rep: *I don't think I can physically pursue many more opportunities because I'm already working as hard as I possibly can. I suppose I'll need to go after bigger deals.*

Manager: *Good. So how would you go about doing that?*

Rep: *I could focus on selling our premium product line, since it's priced about 50% higher than our other products [another Sales Objective].*

Manager: *I like the idea. So what do you need to do over the next month or so to get larger deals in your pipeline?*

Rep: *I need to stop calling on smaller companies and redirect my prospecting effort toward bigger ones [a Sales Activity], probably companies with more than $100 million in revenue, because they're the ones that find real value in our more sophisticated products.*

Manager: *I think that sounds like a great plan. Can we set a goal to have 50% of your pipeline in premium products with companies larger than $100 million by the end of next quarter?*

Rep: *Sure. I think that's doable.*

Manager: *Super. Go get 'em.*

In this second conversation, the sales manager didn't just tell the salesperson to "get more Results," she helped the rep think through which Sales Objectives were most likely to get them the Results and what changes in Sales Activities were required to achieve them. This transition from management by results to management of activities is how sales managers take control of their sales force's performance. Management stops begging for outcomes and starts directing the behaviors that will cause a chain reaction from Activities to Objectives to Results.

We therefore need to take our examination down a level, to explore how Sales Objectives can help us drive toward our desired Business Results.

We had now begun to dig into the management code by examining the level of metrics that cannot be managed whatsoever, Business Results. Eventually, these metrics all fell into one of three categories:

1. **Financial**, which are primary accounting measures like Revenue and Profit (note that these can be reported as either forecasted or realized dollars)
2. **Satisfaction**, which are measures of customer and employee pleasure with certain aspects of a company, its products and services, or its relationships (aka the applause-o-meter)
3. **Market Share**, which are measures of a company's captured portion of its total addressable market

These metrics on the war room wall are really measures of overall corporate health: how healthy the company considers itself, how healthy key stakeholders find it, and how healthy it looks in comparison to its peers. In sum, they determine how well a company is doing. If you have lots of happy, profitable customers, then you are doing well, for sure.

Our examination of Business Results led us to realize that the true nature of a metric is determined by its intended use. Using this conclusion, we eliminated our troublesome Sales Pipeline category entirely and redistributed those metrics to other spots on the wall. If the pipeline metrics were used to forecast financial performance, then into the Financial category of Business Results they went. If they were intended to measure a salesperson's effectiveness in moving deals through the pipeline, then they were diverted to Sales Objectives.

Of course, as high-level corporate outcomes, Business Results cannot be directly managed. To exert any form of control over these numbers, leadership needs to select the right Sales Objectives and manage the right Sales Activities to drive its desired outcomes. See Figure 3.9. We therefore turned our attention to the next challenge in engineering a cohesive set of management metrics—understanding how to identify and measure relevant Sales Objectives.

BUSINESS RESULT	DEFINITION	SAMPLE METRICS IN STUDY
Financial	An accounting-related measure of revenue or profit	• $ Revenue • % Revenue Growth
Satisfaction	The customers' or employees' perception of a company overall or of a specific aspect of the company's products, services, or relationships	• Customer Satisfaction Rating • Employee Satisfaction Index
Market Share	Percentage of targeted market opportunity that has been captured by the company	• % Market Share • Market Penetration

FIGURE 3.9

Business Results with Corresponding Metrics

Sales Objectives— the Sales Force's Mandates

CHAPTER 4

SMILE . . . FOR A WHILE

Business Results, Sales Objectives, Sales Activities, causal links, reverse-engineering—does sales management have to be so complex? No, not always. But as an organization grows and the demands on its sales force expand, sales management necessarily becomes a more sophisticated endeavor. Otherwise, the sales force can't execute the company's go-to-market strategy with precision. Let us explore an example of how such complexity evolves from the simplest beginnings.

Imagine for a moment that you are a young entrepreneur named Griffin. You have just invented a wonderful new device that you believe will revolutionize workplace environments around the world. Your new contraption attaches to commercial ventilation systems and injects a tiny amount of a harmless, nontoxic gas into the air that causes office workers to experience a temporary boost in both their energy and happiness. In addition to creating a more pleasant working environment, it can boost worker productivity by up to 25%. You name your revolutionary product the "Smile-a-While."

Soon you have a new business card with "CEO" stamped on it. Now all you need is a business. As your first executive decision, you choose to hire a salesperson in New York City and turn him loose in search of some revenue. The response is outrageous. Within the first month, he sells 50 Smile-a-While units, and you are getting dozens of calls a day from businesses that want to purchase your workforce productivity device. The revenue starts to flow, and your new business is up and running.

Over the next year, you experience incredible demand for the Smile-a-While. As your salesperson becomes overwhelmed, you hire four more sellers to follow up on leads in the New York area. You also decide to focus on what you have found to be the ideal customers for the Smile-a-While—owners of very large office buildings. The orders come in as fast as you can handle them, and your company continues to grow.

At this point, your sales force is pretty easy to manage. In fact, it's so simple that you've been doing it yourself. Every week your salespeople receive a bunch of leads, they filter through them to find the owners of big office buildings in the city, and then they go out and close deals. With very little involvement from you, your sales force quickly conquers the New York market. There are smiles all around, but things are about to get more complex.

You decide that it's time to really grow your sales force. Having captured all of the prime targets in New York City, you want to deploy additional salespeople into other major cities around the world. But how many salespeople do you need? And how would you most efficiently assign them to geographic territories? Though you've made a good amount of money over the past year, the size of the investment required to deploy such a sales force demands that you do so in a thoughtful, deliberate fashion. Too few sellers in a major city, and you'll be missing opportunities. Too many sellers in one location, and they'll be stepping all over one another, wasting your money as they go. Deploying the optimal sales force is going to be tricky.

In addition to your questions about the efficient deployment of your sales force, you also have concerns about hiring the type of salespeople that can most effectively sell your product.

You've noticed over the past year that two of your sellers have been much more effective than the others in selling the Smile-a-While. If you're going to hire hundreds of salespeople to work in distant locations, you need to make certain that you're hiring the right people with the right skills. This might even be more important than determining how many salespeople to hire. Realizing that you are an inventor and not a sales force expert, you decide to hire a vice president of sales to help build and grow your sales force.

Your VP of sales, Avery, ends up being a real ace. Over the next 24 months, she successfully deploys hundreds of capable salespeople and managers in major cities across the globe. Because of this large and effective sales force, you quickly have Smile-a-Whiles installed in most of the world's big office buildings. But you soon discover that success demands more success.

Though you've made a small fortune, you have also taken on some investors, and they are clamoring for continued growth. To help with this challenge, you decide to hire a vice president of marketing to expand the company's focus. After extensive market analysis, your new VP concludes that the next logical opportunity lies in capturing smaller customers. If you are to continue to grow your company at such a fast rate, you must move down-market and also target the owners of mid-sized office buildings. This seems like a solid strategy, but targeting a new segment of customers will come with some practical hurdles.

The current model of the Smile-a-While is designed to work in large office buildings only, which is why it has been such a success with the owners of these big structures. To succeed with this new type of customer, you will have to develop an additional product line that is suited for smaller ventilation systems. Being a brilliant inventor, you gladly accept the challenge and set to the task of designing a Smile-a-While for mid-sized office buildings. Within six months, the new Grin-Again product line is ready to launch.

It's now been four whirlwind years since you invented the Smile-a-While. As you sit in a large conference room and reflect on your very first year as CEO, you can't help but wish things were that simple again. You had one product, one target customer, one salesperson, and ample revenue pouring in the door. Now you have multiple product lines, multiple target customers, a global sales force, and investors to whom you've promised increasing revenue growth. This is getting even trickier.

Despite the complexities, the Grin-Again product launch is critical to your company's future, and it *must* go well. But several vital decisions beckon:

- How much bigger must your sales force become?
- Will it be capable of selling both product lines?
- How will you ensure that the right customers are being targeted?
- How will you get your sales force to sell the right products?

You didn't face these decisions four years ago when you only managed a single salesperson with a single task. A slight grimace appears on your face, defying the harmless, nontoxic gas that bellows from your building's Smile-a-While unit. Alas, you long for the good ol' days when all you needed was a little revenue.

BEHOLD, THE SALES OBJECTIVE

So this is how sales management becomes complex. As companies grow and their go-to-market strategies become more sophisticated, it is no longer sufficient to simply hire any salesperson, call on any customer, and sell any product. Some customers are better than others, some products are better than others, and as we all know, some salespeople are better than others. Deliberate action is required.

We were working with a client recently, and one of its very tenured sales managers was lamenting the evolution of his organization. Perhaps you've heard similar tales of woe:

When I started working here 30 years ago, my manager handed me a phone book and said, "There's the phone. Go make some sales."

Now we've got high- and low-priority customers, marketing is constantly pushing some new product on us, we make our reps enter a bunch of information into a computer, we're expected to measure this and measure that. It's just crazy.

To which we replied, "Great." It's better to be crazy than stupid. Or even worse, broke.

In the twenty-first century, the only companies that can manage their sales forces with a phone book are the ones that have just started their businesses and the ones that will soon be out of business. Hiring the right salespeople, deploying them in the right way, targeting the right customers, and selling the right products is the only formula for long-term organizational health. The question that each organization has to answer for itself is, What does *right* mean for you?

Some companies will succeed by targeting large customers, and others will succeed by targeting small ones. Some companies will succeed by selling premium products, and others will succeed with more basic offerings. Some companies need big sales forces, others need small ones. Some companies require highly skilled sellers, others don't. There are many paths to success, and history has shown that the only companies that necessarily fail are the ones that try to do it all—whether intentionally or not.

And this is why we need Sales Objectives. They help sales forces evolve from brute force, phone book–guided masses into efficient, strategically focused experts. They lead organizations down the most direct path to their desired Business Results by giving their sales forces the who, what, when, and where of selling. Success is no longer found in making *enough* sales calls to reach your quota. That is a trial-and-error marathon that you may or may not win. Success is now found in making the *right* sales calls to achieve the *right* Sales Objectives to reach your quota—a quicker and more predictable path to the winner's circle.

To illustrate the power of Sales Objectives and their associated metrics as management tools, let us revisit our workplace productivity company. This time, you are Avery, the vice president of sales. You met last week with Griffin, who was quite distraught. Under intense pressure from the board of directors, he had reluctantly committed to doubling revenues over the next three years. Accordingly, he is expecting you to grow sales by at least 25% annually during that time. You give careful consideration to how you should manage your sales force through this growth, and you decide that "management by results" is your best strategy. You schedule a call with all of your sales managers to set the stage and to communicate your expectations.

> Thank you all for joining me on the call today. I met with our CEO last week, and I wanted to communicate to you as quickly as possible a change in our revenue targets going forward. We've set a goal to double our revenues within the next three years, which means that each of you will now have to grow your territories by 25% year over year.
>
> I know this is substantially more than we'd committed to delivering, but we think it is doable. On our side, we have a global base of installed customers and our new Grin-Again product line, which is priced substantially lower than Smile-a-While. Given your past successes and the strength of your teams, I know you will work hard and achieve these new goals. As always, you have my support in every way. Good luck.

The message has been communicated loud and clear: the sales managers have to find a way to grow revenue by 25% a year. How they achieve this result is up to them, but they'd better get there regardless. So what are the managers supposed to tell their sales reps to do? Let's see how a few of the sales managers answer this question for themselves as they hang up their phones:

Manager 1: *Wow, 25% revenue growth? Wow. Well, no use whining about it—let's think about how I'm going to do this. It's pretty clear that we're not going to grow like that selling the cheaper Grin-Again product. We'd have to sell twice as many of those over the next year as we would Smile-a-Whiles. I'm going to need my* sales reps to focus almost exclusively on driving Smile-a-While sales. Otherwise, we'll never get there from here.

Manager 2: Wow, 25% revenue growth? Geez. Well, no use whining about it. I think Avery was right—the installed customer base is probably the path of least resistance to making this happen. I wonder if we could approach our current Smile-a-While customers about switching to Grin-Agains? Some of them could probably get by with the lower capacity. For that matter, they could buy two Grin-Agains and still save money over a full Smile-a-While upgrade. That's it. That's how we'll get there from here. We'll ride Grin-Agains all the way to the bank.

Manager 3: Wow, 25% revenue growth? I should have seen this coming. The corporate office is always upping the ante for us guys in the field. Now, how am I going to make this happen? If 25% is the growth target, then I guess they're expecting us to work 25% harder. I'll have to send my reps calling on prospects farther outside of their cities, but I think I can dig up 25% more leads than we're feeding them now. It's gonna be tough, but we'll all just have to grind it out.

Three different sales managers, and three different strategies. One will neglect the new product line, one will cannibalize the current product line, and a third will just grind it out. Hmm. It's not looking good for Griffin. He might have some explaining to do to his board of directors, as his sales force muddles through the next three years.

Perhaps there is a way that Avery could have avoided this unfocused selling effort by providing her managers with a little more guidance in the form of thoughtful Sales Objectives. Let's give her one more conference call to send her people down the right path:

Thank you all for joining the call today. When we spoke last week, I shared with you our new revenue targets for the next three years. I want to follow up with you regarding the path that we believe will get us there most quickly and most likely.

You all have done a fantastic job over the last several years in selling Smile-a-Whiles into most of the large office space around *the world. Consequently, we already have 80% of the segment as customers, and we don't believe that the remaining 20% is fertile enough ground for us to reach our goals by concentrating solely on large customers. While we can't ignore that segment, we will need to shift our focus to the owners of smaller buildings that are perfectly suited for our new Grin-Again product line.*

We have set an objective for next year to get 30% of our revenue from the Grin-Again line of products. The following two years, we would like to see that number increase to 40% and 50%, respectively. I trust that each of you will adjust your selling activities appropriately to target smaller customers in whatever portion you believe will get you to these product-mix objectives.

Also, your reps will receive training on the new product line within the next 90 days, which should help with this transition. And I would like for each of you to provide me with a 12-month hiring plan that you think is reasonable.

Hopefully this call has provided you with a little more direction and confidence that we can attain our desired outcomes. Thank you again.

Unlike the panic-inducing first call, all three managers will leave this conversation with the exact same Sales Objective—to get 30% of their revenues next year from the Grin-Again product line. They also know that they must shift sufficient selling effort toward smaller customers in order to hit that number. Further, they will schedule product training for their reps and determine how much additional selling capacity is needed to reach their three-year growth targets. Sounds like a good plan.

This is how powerful clearly stated Sales Objectives are in driving sales force behaviors that are aligned with corporate goals. Sales Objectives are often the missing link between what the leadership team wants and what the sales force does. Without cogent Sales Objectives, the sales force does the best it can. With cogent Sales Objectives, the sales force does what it *should*.

So one school of sales management says to just tell your salespeople the results you expect and then trust them to deliver. In other words, "We need 25% growth in revenues, please. Let us know if we can help." This management style is certainly easier than charting a predefined path for your sales force, and some managers and sellers may even prefer it, because it gives them the freedom to define their own strategy. However, it's hard to argue that it's the best approach to drive consistent execution in the field that you *know* will lead most directly to your goals. It's the equivalent of saying, "There is the finish line. Feel free to take as many suboptimal paths there as you like to get there. But run fast!"

Our school of thought says to tell them the results you expect, tell them the objectives that will get them there, and then trust them to execute. In other words, "We need 25% growth in revenues, and here is what you need to do to accomplish that." If I were a VP of sales wanting more control over field-level activity, then I would prefer this approach. If I were a sales manager wanting a clear path to success, I would also prefer this approach. And if I were a salesperson wanting to avoid the pain of trial-and-error selling, I would strongly prefer this approach. It's the equivalent of, "There is the finish line, and here is the shortest route to get there." Behold the power of the Sales Objective.

STUFF FOR SALES MANAGEMENT TO WORRY ABOUT

As we discussed, Business Results are the outcomes of an entire organization's collective efforts. If a company has enough happy customers to meet its financial expectations, life is good for everyone. No single corporate function can take credit for the health of the entity, but every part of the business must contribute. That is, each part of the organization has objectives that it must achieve in order for the company to attain its high-level Business Results.

For example, manufacturing's objectives might include producing enough products to satisfy customer demand. Marketing might be accountable for developing new products that are relevant for its target markets. Finance might be tasked with

Market Coverage
Maintaining sufficient selling capacity to pursue all desired opportunities

Sales Force Capability
Developing a sales force that is able to effectively execute its selling activities

Customer Focus
Capturing, retaining, and growing the customers your company wants to have

Product Focus
Selling the products and services your company wants to sell

FIGURE 4.1

The Sales Objectives

maintaining sufficient capital to operate the business. Across the company, every department has critical business objectives that are specific to its functional domain.

Sales, of course, has its own set of management objectives. They are sales' contributions to the company's overall Business Results and are the guideposts that the sales force should use to align its day-to-day selling activities. When we studied the metrics on our wall, we found that four distinct categories of Sales Objectives emerged (see Figure 4.1).

First, there is a group of metrics that we labeled *Market Coverage*. These metrics measure the objective of having enough salespeople in the right places to cover all of a company's desired prospects and customers. A sales force must be the right size and shape in order to fully execute its go-to-market strategy.

The second set of metrics we found is meant to assess what we call *Sales Force Capability*. These metrics quantify the objective of having effective salespeople who can competently sell your products to your target customers. If there is sufficient

Market Coverage *and* the sellers are highly capable, then the company has a very potent sales force indeed.

Third is a collection of metrics that measures Customer Focus. These metrics evaluate the objective of attracting, retaining, and growing the types of customers that the organization wants. Whether the company wants to focus on new customers, existing customers, or some other demographic profile, these measures provide the sales force with guidance on which customers to pursue.

Finally, we observed a category of metrics about Product Focus. These metrics measure the objective of selling the products and services that the company prefers to sell. Whether they are products with higher profit margins or they have some other strategic value, these metrics focus the sales force on selling the right things.

In sum, these four Sales Objectives and their associated metrics help answer the questions our young entrepreneur posed as he tried to position his company for growth:

- Do I have enough salespeople in the right places?
- Are they capable sellers?
- Are they targeting the right customers?
- Are they selling the right products?

It is worth restating that Sales Objectives cannot be directly managed; they must be influenced by directing Sales Activities. For instance, you cannot immediately have more salespeople, but you can begin recruiting additional head count. You cannot command your salespeople to have more skill, but you can send them to training. You cannot instantly have more new customers, but you can ask your salespeople to make more prospecting calls. And you cannot will your current product mix to change, but you can propose certain products more frequently in your sales calls. Therefore, setting the right Sales Objectives provides sales managers with critical directions on how they should manage their salespeople's daily activities. See Figure 4.2.

It's also worth noting that sales management does not always get to choose the specific Sales Objectives for which it is held

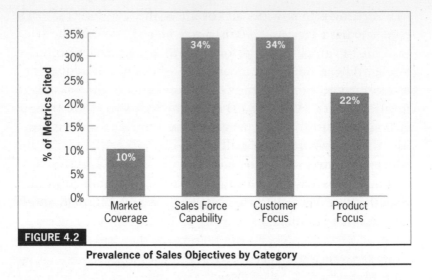

FIGURE 4.2

Prevalence of Sales Objectives by Category

accountable. Often marketing and senior executives have the heavier hand in identifying the "right" customers to target and the "right" products to sell. However, once the Sales Objectives are determined and the performance targets are set, the responsibility for achieving the objectives falls squarely on sales management.

This fact was phrased perfectly by a client of ours. We were training a team of its sales managers on how to use the concepts in this book to improve coaching interactions, and one of the VPs of sales happened to walk in as we were discussing Sales Objectives. He glanced at the metrics on the board and immediately blurted out, "Hey, that's all the stuff that I worry about!" Yes, it is true—this is the stuff that good sales management should worry about.

THE SALES FORCE AS GROUND COVER

Companies have tried for decades to clearly define the relationship between their sales and marketing functions. One definition that we found interesting proposes that the role of marketing is to provide "air cover" for the sales force. If that's the case, then I guess it's fair to consider the role of the sales force to be "ground cover" for marketing. Whatever products marketing conjures up at a company's corporate headquarters, its salespeople will find a way to sell in their far-flung sales territories. But it's crucial that the sales force has the right troops, in the right numbers, in the right places to fight and win each battle. Otherwise, trouble will ensue.

Appropriately, we found a category of Sales Objective metrics that is used to measure just those dimensions of a sales organization. We called this category *Market Coverage*, and it includes these numbers:

- Percentage of Market Opportunity Covered
- Percentage of Target Prospects Contacted
- Percentage of Productive Time for Reps
- Percentage of Vacant Positions

In essence, these metrics all point to one vital question for sales management: does your company have enough salespeople engaging the right customers to accomplish its go-to-market strategy? Or stated differently, is there enough selling effort in place to capture all of your potential opportunity in the marketplace? Too much effort, and your cost of sale is high. Too little effort, and your revenue underperforms. Spend the effort on the wrong customers, and resources are wasted. Finding the right coverage model is a key to optimizing sales force productivity.

The objective of the Market Coverage sales metrics is *to help make staffing and time allocation adjustments that will keep your sales force operating at peak productivity.*

There are many different ways to measure your level of selling effort. Company-wide, you could calculate it as the aggregate number of hours your sales force has to make sales calls, say 60,000 hours per year across all of your salespeople. You might also examine it at an individual level, like 6 hours of productive time each day per salesperson. You could even measure it from a customer's perspectives, for instance, each of your customers

AVAILABLE EFFORT
- Time to Hire
- Time to Productivity
- Ramp-Up Time
- Percentage Selling Time
- Percentage Customer-Facing Time
- Number of Total Selling Hours
- Percentage Undesired Attrition
- Turnover Rate

- Sales Rep Turnover
- Salesperson Attrition
- Attrition Rate
- Head Count Variance

ACCURACY OF EFFORT
- Sales Coverage Accuracy
- Percentage of Customers Contacted
- Percentage of Prospects Called
- Coverage Gaps

EFFICIENCY OF EFFORT
- Cost per Call
- Cost of Sale as Percentage of Revenue
- Cost of Sale
- Total Cost of Sale

Companies with at Least One Such Metric

32%

FIGURE 4.3

Sales Objective Metrics in Our Study: Market Coverage

is contacted 12 times a year. However you choose to analyze it, Market Coverage metrics attempt to gauge when you have enough sales force to do what you want to do. See Figure 4.3.

To examine how Market Coverage metrics might be used in practice, let's revisit the tale of our CEO and vice president of sales. It has now been one year since they announced their new growth targets, and they are meeting to review progress against their desired Business Result of a 25% increase in revenue.

Griffin: *Avery, I have to tell you that I'm very pleased with our revenue growth this year. It's almost hard to believe that we were able to grow our revenue by 30%.*

Avery: *Yes, things have mostly gone according to plan. And trust me, we did lots of planning.*

Griffin: *I know that you and your team have been practically trapped in your war room most of the year. What did you find to be the key drivers of your success?*

Avery: *Well, there have been a lot of contributing factors, but most of the growth came from the launch of our new Grin-Again product line.*

Griffin: *Oh sure, those numbers were spectacular.*

Avery: *Yes, but there was a lot of stuff to worry about during the launch. Probably our biggest concern was getting the sales* force to the right size to both sustain our Smile-a-While sales and launch the Grin-Again.

Griffin: I remember that you requested a lot of new head count.

Avery: Getting the right amount of selling effort in the field was absolutely critical if we were going to make this happen. There was no margin for a trial-and-error approach.

Griffin: Agreed.

Avery: I don't know if you recall, but we had some pretty clear sales force objectives that guided our actions. For instance, we wanted to make at least one sales call on 25% of the addressable market for Grin-Agains every 120 days after the launch. Therefore, Percentage of Grin-Again Prospects Contacted per Quarter became a key number on our war room wall.

Griffin: Hmm. You weren't just reporting progress against the revenue goal? You were actually tracking the number of calls that you made on certain types of customers?

Avery: Absolutely. It was essential to ensure that we were covering our market properly. If we didn't make enough calls on the right types of customers, it wouldn't matter how skilled our salespeople are or how wonderful the Grin-Again is. We could've never hit our revenue number. So we asked each of our reps to make 10 Grin-Again prospecting calls each week.

Griffin: That's really smart. I knew there was a reason we hired you.

Avery: Well, we didn't stop there. We had to set a couple of other objectives for the sales force in order to make those calls. For instance, we calculated that we needed to hire 10 sales reps every 30 days in order to grow our head count sufficiently. Therefore, another important metric on the wall was Percentage of Job Openings Filled per Month. And finally, we really couldn't afford much sales force attrition during this time, so we also kept a very sharp eye on Percentage of Involuntary Turnover per Quarter. We wanted that number to stay below 10%. By getting enough selling effort in place to make enough calls on enough prospects, we gave ourselves at least a fighting chance to hit our goals. If we hadn't tracked those key Sales Objectives, it's unlikely that our attention would've been focused on getting the Market Coverage correct. We would have just stared at

Griffin: *Avery, I'll say it again: I knew there was a reason we hired you.*

The VP of sales was exactly correct in her assertion that having enough of the right selling effort in the right places is foundational to success. If your sales force doesn't have sufficient hours in the day to do what it needs to do, then it's fighting a losing battle. We once analyzed a client's sales force that was falling dramatically short of expectations, and we discovered that its head count was *half* the size it needed to be in order to make its desired volume of sales calls. No surprise, then, that its salespeople were both exhausted and frustrated. They didn't have a fighting chance.

We suspect that many sales leaders find themselves in the unfortunate position of trying to perform Herculean feats with undersized sales forces. In fact, we've seen data suggesting that *most* sales forces are understaffed to execute their go-to-market strategies. We don't know whether or not that is true, but our research did reveal one thing for certain: most sales forces don't know either.

Market Coverage metrics were the least prominent of the Sales Objectives measurements in our research. Whether it is because the numbers are difficult to calculate, or whether it's too enticing to just allocate head count based on intuition, these numbers are missing from most war room walls. It's a shame, because these metrics would be extremely useful for leadership.

If these metrics *were* on the wall, it would be easier for sales management to staff its sales forces appropriately. Companies could get the greatest possible revenue at the least possible cost by fine-tuning their ground cover to fit the market opportunity. Managers could make informed decisions at the Sales Activity level that could dramatically affect Sales Objectives and Business Results. If your company doesn't collect Market Coverage metrics, just imagine what you might be missing. Or stated more accurately, imagine which customers you might be missing.

THE "CAPABLE"
SALES FORCE

We just stated that getting the right number of salespeople in front of the right customers is a foundation of sales success. However, to build on that foundation, you need sellers who know what to do once they *are* in front of the customer. When an unqualified seller meets a qualified prospect, it's not only a waste of time for the buyer. It's a waste of resources for the sales force.

The second type of Sales Objective metric we found in our research is therefore intended to prevent such disastrous consequences. Measures of Sales Force Capability are intended to answer the specific question, *Are my salespeople capable of doing what they need to do?* Sales Force Capability metrics include numbers like these:

- Deal Win/Loss Ratio
- Percentage of Deals Advancing by Stage
- Length of the Sales Cycle
- Salesperson Competency Index

Unlike measures of Market Coverage, nearly every organization has these numbers on their wall. This is because of the obvious and direct linkage between the capability of a sales force and the achievement of its desired Business Results. If you close more deals, you get more revenue. If you can shorten the sales cycle, then you get that revenue even faster. These are very powerful metrics, for sure.

At first glance, the term *capability* might seem to refer to the skill level of a sales force, and skills are typically the first lever that sales management pulls to boost Sales Force Capability. If salespeople don't seem "capable" of winning enough deals, then off to a training class they go. And while the skill of the salesperson is unquestionably an important determinant of his success, Sales Force Capability is affected by many more things than just selling skills.

Capability is a measure of the sales force's overall effectiveness in accomplishing its goals.[1] This is influenced by the strategies the salespeople employ, the processes they are told to follow, the tools they are given to support their activities, the expectations that are communicated to them, and many other sales management decisions that go well beyond the scope of training to develop sheer selling skills. We too often see management relying on only two levers to drive sales performance—training and incentive compensation—but Sales Force Capability is most forcefully influenced by applying pressure from many different directions. So while these measures do point to the underlying skill of the sales force, management has many ways to affect the capability of its sellers.

There are three interesting characteristics about this category of Sales Objective. First, very few companies in our study attempted to gauge Sales Force Capability by measuring skill or knowledge directly. Whether for the reason just stated or because skills can be difficult to quantify, we observed only a few related metrics, like Comprehension of Product Knowledge or Demonstrated Selling Skills. Most often, companies chose to judge their salespeople's capabilities by the outcomes of the sellers' effort. Metrics such as Close Rates or Conversion Ratios Between Stages were used to assess the overall abilities of a sales force, incorporating the impacts of sales training, selling processes, supporting tools, and other influencers.

Second, there is no objective benchmark for excellence. Unlike Market Coverage, for which the goal is clearly to cover 100% of your targeted customers, it's unrealistic to expect your sales force to close 100% of its deals. So what, then, would you consider to be an excellent Deal Win Rate? Should your sales force win 75% of the deals it pursues? Or 50%? Or 35%? Who knows? These numbers are only relative to your own sales force's past performance. Your threshold for "good" must come from within.

---

1. Note that we considered labeling this category of metrics "Sales Effectiveness." However, the term *sales effectiveness* has become so common and is used in so many different ways, we felt it would come with excess baggage.

Finally, you *always* want *all* of these metrics to be improving. With a different Sales Objective like Product Focus, you may set an objective this year to obtain 30% of your revenue from a new line of products, and then next year you may *intentionally lower* your target to 20% as your product strategy shifts. However, you *never* want your Deal Win Rate to drop from 30% to 20%. Never. You always want more deals to advance and your skill level to increase. You always want your sales cycle to shorten. You always want your Sales Force Capability metrics to move in the same direction. This is a classic case of continuous improvement as the goal. So while there is no clear destination for any of these numbers, you always know which direction you want to be headed. See Figure 4.4.

To view these numbers in action, let's return to Griffin and Avery. It is now 12 months later, and they have just completed year two of their three-year growth plan. Griffin comes striding into Avery's office.

Griffin: *Avery, I just saw the final numbers for this fiscal year's revenue. We totally destroyed the target! Congratulations on yet another great performance by your sales team.*

Avery: *Thank you, boss. I have to admit that even I was surprised by how far we blew past our 25% growth goal. I can't say enough good things about our sales force—and in particular our frontline sales managers. They worked really hard this year, and even more importantly, they worked smart.*

Griffin: *What do you mean, they worked smart?*

Avery: *Well, as you recall, our big challenge last year was Market Coverage. We needed to get enough salespeople on board quickly enough to target the new Grin-Again prospects. Don't get me wrong, we hired good people, but last year's success was largely obtained through brute force.*

Griffin: *So what was your secret to success this year?*

Avery: *This year was all about improving our salespeople's ability to sell the Grin-Again most effectively. In other words, we really focused on developing our Sales Force Capability.*

Griffin: *Ah, interesting. So that's why you conducted all of that sales training this past year.*

SKILL/KNOWLEDGE
- Comprehension of Product Information
- Demonstrated Selling Skills
- Percentage of Salespeople Meeting Development Goals
- Increased Skill Index from Training
- Improvement in Specific Skills
- Competency Assessment Index
- Average Tenure of Rep
  (Note: Research shows that tenure is only loosely correlated with performance.)

OVERALL EFFECTIVENESS
- Close Rate (4)
- Win/Loss Ratio (2)
- Average Close Ratio
- Win/Loss Rate
- Percentage of Deals Won
- Causes of Lost Deals
- Number of Deals Completed per Salesperson
- Sales per Call

SALES CYCLE ADVANCEMENT
- Percentage Deals Advancing by Stage (2)
- Pipeline Realization Rate
- Percentage of Forecasted Deals That Close
- Percentage of Deals in Each Stage
- Revenue by Stage of the Sales Cycle per Rep
- Proposal Win Rates
- Customer Conversion Rates by Stage
- Number of Deals by Stage per Rep
- Stages with Greatest Failure to Advance
- Percentage Opportunities Within Stages
- Conversion Ratios Between Stages
- Call Outcomes
- Pipeline Aging by Stage
- Number of Meetings (2)
- Number of Appointments
- Number of Product Evaluations

- Number of New Proposals
- Sales Cycle Time (3)
- Length of Sales Cycle
- Days to Complete Sales Cycle
- Days Sales Cycle Time
- Average Sales Cycle

PRICING/ NEGOTIATING
- Price Realization
- Pricing Effectiveness by Rep
- Change in Negotiated Price
- Percentage of Deals Sold at Discount
- Average Discount Level
- Negotiated Margins

MANAGER
- Coaching Quality Index
- Quality of Coaching
- Forecast Accuracy (4)
- Manager's Forecast Accuracy

Companies with at Least One Such Metric

74%

FIGURE 4.4

Sales Objective Metrics in Our Study: Sales Force Capability

Avery: *Yes, there was a lot of training, but there was also much more. First we had to set some appropriate Sales Objectives so our sales managers had something to shoot for. We analyzed our Close Rates and discovered that although we had historically converted around 40% of our Smile-a-While leads, we won only 25% of our Grin-Again deals during its first year in the market. So, we figured there was room to improve our salespeople's capabilities with the Grin-Again sales. Our* objective for this year was to raise our Grin-Again Close Rates to 40%—bringing it up to par with the Smile-a-While.

Griffin: *Makes sense.*

Avery: *Yep. We also did a little more investigation and discovered that our Grin-Again deals were actually proceeding through the sales cycle just fine until our proposals went out the door.*

Griffin: *What do you mean?*

Avery: *For some reason, our Proposal Win Rate was much lower with the Grin-Again than with the Smile-a-While. So we set a separate Sales Objective to win 60% of all proposals that were submitted to Grin-Again prospects.*

Griffin: *Huh. So how'd you go about increasing your Proposal Win Rate and overall Close Rate with the Grin-Again?*

Avery: *We had to change quite a few things in our Sales Activities. As you pointed out, we did a bunch of training and coaching this year, but it was very focused on how to write a winning Grin-Again proposal. We also found that we needed a simpler proposal and contract for the smaller Grin-Again customers. Therefore, we developed a proposal template to help reps create better documents. Finally, we created a proposal review process so the sales managers could help the reps with quality control of all outgoing proposals. By the end of the year, our Proposal Win Rate went to 65%, which led to an overall Close Rate of 45%. And that's how we destroyed our target last year.*

Griffin: *Sales Force Capability, eh? Sounds like good stuff.*

Avery: *Yes. It is good stuff. Hard stuff to do, but great for the sales force.*

As Griffin's ace VP of sales pointed out, having the right people in the right place is only the first of many challenges for crafty sales leaders. Next, they have to make certain that their salespeople are prepared to do the right things. And that is the role of Sales Force Capability metrics—to make sure that your sellers are capable of doing the right things. Generating leads, advancing opportunities, and closing deals are at the heart of a salesperson's role. You need to know that your salespeople can execute such activities effectively.

One final observation regarding Sales Force Capability is the significant impact that frontline sales managers have on these metrics. While sales managers can influence all of the Sales Objectives in this chapter, the manager is uniquely able to improve a salesperson's capability. Frontline sales managers are often the only people with the frequent access to sellers that is required to reinforce training, provide guidance, deliver coaching, ensure tool usage, and all the other activities that affect Sales Force Capability.

In fact, we found a handful of metrics in our research that evaluate the capabilities of managers themselves. Measures like Coaching Quality Index reveal how capably managers are developing their salespeople. We hope that the prevalence of manager-focused metrics increases as sales manager development becomes an organizational priority.

ACQUIRE, RETAIN, GROW, REPEAT

Management guru Peter Drucker famously wrote that there is only one valid purpose for any business: to create a customer.[2] This may be true, but anyone reading this book knows that there's a little more to it than that. Customers cannot simply be created. They have to be identified, courted, and won. The level of effort required to perform these tasks necessitates focus on the part of a sales force. Time spent courting one customer is time *not* spent courting another. Since not all customers are equally desirable, sales management must be directive about where its salespeople are investing their time. Our study of sales force metrics revealed a category of Sales Objectives dedicated to this very decision.

Customer Focus measures point a company's sales force in the direction of its most desired customers. They provide insight into how successfully your salespeople are acquiring,

2. Peter Drucker, *The Practice of Management* (New York: Harper & Brothers, 1954).

retaining, and growing the types of customers that will lead to the achievement of your ultimate Business Results. The Customer Focus category includes these customer-centric metrics:

- Revenue from New Customers
- Revenue Growth from Key Accounts
- Customer Retention Rates
- Revenue per Customer Segment
- Share of Wallet

Not surprisingly, many of the metrics in this category were intended to measure success in acquiring new customers. New customer acquisition is a logical obsession for sales leadership, since it is the most intuitive path to growth. There is something magical about acquiring a new customer, and salespeople who have a particular knack for winning new customers are often treated as enigmatic heroes. Despite the fact that the cost of pursuing new accounts typically makes them much less profitable than existing customers, it is quite clear from our research that sales leaders regard new customers with very great affection.

Beyond distinguishing between new and existing customers, many companies in our study also set objectives to target customers with specific characteristics. These might be prospects of a certain size, in a certain industry, from a certain geographic region, or grouped any other way that potential customers can be segmented. Steering your sales force toward a particular customer segment can be a very effective way to increase win rates and boost profitability, since some customers are easier to engage and more likely to buy than others. We have seen Customer Focus objectives drive dramatic improvement in sales performance by shepherding misguided salespeople off the path of least resistance and into a target-rich environment.

Of course, many companies thrive by nurturing ongoing relationships with their existing customers. If acquiring new customers or moving into new customer segments is not a viable growth strategy, then maximizing the value of existing accounts becomes a critical Sales Objective. Measures such as Share of Wallet or Revenue Growth from Key Accounts become a focal point for the sales force, as it works to embed itself deeper and wider inside each of its accounts. All other things being equal, wooing existing customers is both easier and cheaper than courting total strangers.

We were relieved to see that there is an abundance of metrics in our research directed at customer retention and growth. We have worked with many sales forces that are so obsessed with bringing new business in the front door that they forget to lock the rear exits. One leadership team had set a target to grow its customer base by 15% annually, but it was simultaneously suffering 20% attrition with its existing customers. When we pointed out to its head of sales that his team would have to effectively grow sales by 35% each year to grow its customer base by 15%, we thought an ambulance would need to be called. To avoid such emergencies, numbers like Churn Rate and Customer Retention deserve a very prominent space on any war room wall. See Figure 4.5 for a list of the Customer Focus metrics we found in our study.

To demonstrate the clever use of Customer Focus metrics, let us check in on Griffin and Avery as they close the third and final year of their effort to double the size of their workforce productivity company.

Griffin: *Whew! Avery, I can't believe that we actually did it. Or more appropriately, your team did it. You more than doubled the size of our company in three years. Congratulations once more.*

Avery: *Yeah, I have to say that this was probably the most difficult year of the three. In year one, we focused on getting the Market Coverage right, which was kind of a no-brainer. In year two, we concentrated on improving our Sales Force Capability, which really made a huge impact. But once we had a capable sales force covering our target markets, we really didn't know where year three's revenue growth was hiding.*

Griffin: *We shifted our Customer Focus, didn't we?*

ACQUIRING NEW CUSTOMERS
- Revenue from New Customers (2)
- Customer Acquisition Rate
- Number of New Accounts (2)
- New Accounts
- New Business
- Volume of New Business
- Revenue from New Buying Centers
- New Business from New Clients
- Wins from New Accounts
- Number of New Customers
- Number of New Contacts in CRM

RETAINING AND GROWING EXISTING CUSTOMERS
- Share of Wallet (5)
- Percentage Customer Retention (2)
- Customer Churn Rate (2)
- Revenue Growth in Existing Customers (2)
- Revenue Retention per Account
- Business Retention Rate
- Repeat Customer Rate

- Number of Customers
- Number of Active Accounts
- Duration of Customer Relationship
- Size of Wallet
- Frequency of Purchase
- Average Inter-Purchase Time
- Termination of Unprofitable Customers
- Average Length of Customer Relationship
- Customer Inactivity
- Percentage Customer Reactivation
- Revenue from Existing Customers
- Customer Retention Rates
- Existing Business from Existing Customers
- Percentage of Accounts Retained
- New Business from Existing Customers
- Revenue Growth from Key Accounts
- Revenue from Retained Customers
- Revenue Run Rate per Customer
- Customer Penetration Rate
- Average Customer Profitability

- Account Profitability

CUSTOMER MIX
- Revenue per Customer Segment (2)
- Diversification Across Customers
- Segment Penetration
- Ratio of New/Existing Business
- Percentage in Target Customer Segment
- Customer Penetration by Customer Type
- Percentage of Revenue from Target Markets
- Multinational vs. Domestic Customers
- Revenue by Customer Type
- Revenue by Sales Cycle Stage by Customer Type
- Net Contribution per Segment
- Market Share by Customer Segment
- Number of Meetings by Customer Type

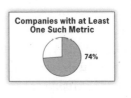

Companies with at Least One Such Metric

74%

Sales Objective Metrics in Our Study: Customer Focus

Avery: *That's right. One of our sales reps came up with the idea that schools would be a great target for the Grin-Again. Teachers can get greater engagement from their students, which leads to higher achievement in nearly every measure of academic performance and fewer disciplinary problems, to boot.*

Griffin: *You know, we probably should have thought of that in the first place. What a perfect customer segment that is.*

Avery: *Absolutely. So we set a Sales Objective to get 30% of year-three revenues from the education segment. Therefore, Grin-Again Revenue by Customer Type became a key metric for the entire team.*

Griffin: *And your salespeople responded.*

Avery: *It was actually more difficult than you might think to get our salespeople focused on schools as their key prospects. Calling on a different type of buyer was challenging, and the sales cycle is longer than in the commercial segments. They really resisted in the beginning, so we had to ride that Customer Focus metric hard. Our sales managers also had to make all kinds of changes to their Sales Activities, such as redesigning territories, retraining reps, etc. We even had to mandate that each rep make a dozen prospecting calls each week. It was a full-scale change-management effort.*

As Avery highlighted, getting salespeople to focus on the right customers can be a challenge. Further, different Customer Focus objectives require different types of execution in the field. Acquiring new customers does not involve the same tasks as growing existing accounts. And targeting an unfamiliar customer segment can demand even more uncomfortable behaviors. Setting the proper Sales Objectives is always crucial, particularly when you're providing your sales force with Customer Focus objectives. Put salespeople in front of the wrong customers to do the wrong stuff, and bad things will happen by design.

SELL SOMETHING . . . BUT NOT JUST ANYTHING

Now you have a sales force that is perfectly sized, highly capable, and totally focused on your ideal customers. The final Sales Objective that you have to communicate is this: what do you want your sellers to sell? Nearly every company has a variety of products and services it can offer to its customers. Some products are new, some are old. Some are high-margin, some are less profitable. Some are designed for specific customer uses, some are more universally applicable.

In our study of sales force metrics, we discovered that most companies are quite deliberate about which products they send their sales forces into the world to sell. Measures of Product Focus include numbers like these:

- Revenue by Product
- Percentage of Revenue from Target Products
- Number of Unique Products Sold per Rep
- Cross-Sell Rate

As you might detect from this short list, there are two primary dimensions to this Sales Objective—product mix and product breadth.

At one level, Product Focus metrics reveal the relative frequency with which each of the company's products is being sold. Also known as *product mix*, these measures can be extremely important for product-driven companies. Such organizations with numerous product lines and frequent new product introductions can see their overall profitability affected dramatically by the types of products that are being sold.

We have one such client that maintains its premium market position and high profit margins through the frequent introduction of new products. As its existing products mature and come under competitive pricing pressure, it launches newer products that are once again differentiated and command a premium price. Its ongoing Sales Objective is to shift sales away from older offerings and toward newer products as quickly as possible. Consequently, its war room wall is covered with Product Focus numbers. If its product mix does not shift quickly enough after a new product introduction, its sales force comes under intense pressure to allocate additional selling effort toward the new offerings. Salespeople are individually measured and compensated based on these product-mix metrics.

Other companies don't have products with such limited shelf lives, but they do have products and services that are complementary to one another in some way. These organizations can be as intensely focused on which products are being sold, however, they view an incumbent product as a point of leverage to sell additional products and services into their customer base. Typically through account planning activities and internal coordination, they hope to cross-sell a broader range of offerings that will increase the overall value of their existing customer relationships.

A classic example of ambitious cross-selling could be seen in the vast diversification of accounting firms in the twentieth century. Starting with tax and audit services, these firms soon discovered that their visibility into their clients' operations positioned them to sell management consulting services as add-ons to their traditional offerings. And as information technology came onto the scene, these firms found that they could further leverage their management relationships into large IT consulting projects. From debits and credits, to business process engineering, to CRM implementations, accounting firms became expert cross-sellers and grew into multibillion-dollar global organizations. If you are a large client of one of these firms, you can rest assured that you are a number on their war room wall, because they maniacally track revenue diversification across their major accounts. As they should.

Using Product Focus as a primary Sales Objective can have an incredible impact on a company's Business Results. Depending on your particular product strategy, providing your sales force with explicit guidance on which products and services to sell can set you on a course to high profitability and revenue growth. Failing to do so will essentially turn each individual salesperson into his own marketing department, setting product strategy for you as he sees fit in the field. See Figure 4.6.

Let us pay one last visit to our friends at the workplace productivity company, where the confetti has settled after their successful three-year Grin-Again sales drive. They are now discussing their next trick to spur additional revenue growth.

PRODUCT SIZE
- Average Deal Size (2)
- Number of Wins Over Certain Size
- Average Contract Size
- Deal Size
- Average Sale Price
- Number of High-Volume Purchases

PRODUCT TYPE
- Revenue by Product (2)
- Revenue Variance by Product
- Number of New Customers by Product Line
- Account Penetration per Product
- Revenue by Supplier
- Percentage of Revenue from Target Products
- Revenue by Product Line

- Revenue by Stage of Sales Cycle by Product Line
- Effective New Product Launch
- Revenue Across Product Sets
- Diversification Across Products (Number of Deals)
- Unit Sales Across Product Sets
- Number of Profitable Products
- Closes by Product Volume
- Revenue by Pipeline Stage by Product (Revenue and Number of Deals)
- Number of Prospects by Product Line
- Product Mix

PRODUCT VOLUME
- Volume (2)
- Number of Units Sold
- Volume per FTE

PRODUCT LEVERAGE
- Up-Selling
- Cross-Selling
- Up-Sell Rate
- Cross-Sell Rate
- Percentage of Cross-Business Unit Sales
- Number of Line Items Sold per Customer
- Unique Products per Account
- Cross-Selling Products
- Number of Unique Products Sold per Rep
- Number of Reps Selling Each Product
- Product Line Extensions

Companies with at Least One Such Metric

58%

FIGURE 4.6

Sales Objective Metrics in Our Study: Product Focus

Avery: Well, boss, we've accomplished all we set out to do three years ago. Where do we go from here?

Griffin: We're going to stay right where we are, inside our existing customer base, and sell them something new.

Avery: Really. You have something up your sleeve that you haven't told me about?

Griffin: Indeed I do. Our development group is ready to launch a new device that can be fitted to any of our existing units. We're calling it the Re-Joys, and it enables the installed unit to be just as effective while running at a lower power setting. Also, it will pay for itself in less than a year through lower energy consumption. It should be an easy sale for your team.

Avery: That does sound easy.

Griffin: *You might be pleased to know that I've learned a thing or two about Sales Objectives by watching you work over the past three years. We're gonna call this the year of Product Focus. I'd like to set two new objectives for your team, if I may. The first key performance indicator will be a Cross-Sell Rate of 50%. That is, I'd like for your team to sell Re-Joys into half of our existing customers this year.*

Avery: *I like it. That should be doable.*

Griffin: *The second is an Attach Rate of 75%. In other words, I hope your salespeople can sell a Re-Joys unit with three-quarters of any new Smile-a-While or Grin-Again sales.*

Avery: *Also doable. Of course, our sales managers will have to once again change some of their Sales Activities—new training, altered call patterns, and so on. But I think this is a great plan.*

Our final Sales Objective of Product Focus completes the lineup of stuff for sales management to worry about. First, you need to ensure that you have enough selling effort to sufficiently cover your target markets. Second, you must develop a sales force capable of effectively selling your products and service. Third, you need to focus them on the right types of customers. And finally, you must provide them with guidance on what types of products to sell. If you meet all of these Sales Objectives, you will have a laser-guided sales force that will destroy your targets as well. And that will put a smile on your face.

THE SALES FORCE: REVENUE MACHINE OR STRATEGIC WEAPON?

In today's information age, it's a rare occurrence when someone poses a question that can't be quickly answered. Any question of fact is just an Internet search away, and any question of opinion can be discharged at will. For a question to really stop you in your tracks, it has to be one that lurks somewhere in-between—a question that begs the facts but is colored by opinion. These are questions that can nag, and nag, and nag.

Several years ago we were speaking with a large financial institution, and its global head of sales posed such a provocative question. His question was simply this:

> ## [How do I know if my sales force is good?]

He went on to explain:

> *I have dozens of sales forces around the world. Sales forces that sell products, sales forces that sell services, sales forces in Europe, sales forces in North America, sales forces that target small business, sales forces that target multinational corporations. But how do I know if any of them are good? Do I judge them by whether or not they meet their quota? In reality, I set their quota, so that's an artificial measure. And the business environments in each region vary dramatically, so their pricing varies, and their products vary. With so many variables in play, how do I know if my sales forces are really any good?*

The sales leader didn't actually expect an answer to his question that day, but he should have. He *should* be able to know if he has a good sales force. That's his job. It's every sales leader's job to build a good sales force. But we would bet that few sales leaders can answer this question with honest confidence. How would you answer this question? How good is *your* sales force?

This question pestered us for quite a while. In fact, it led to some of the original inquiries that inspired the research in this book. Just because a sales force hits its financial targets, does that mean that it's necessarily a great sales force? Of course not. We all know that many sales forces have succeeded because of a knockout product or explosive customer demand. There are dozens of factors that can drag a mediocre sales force beyond its quota. Conversely, a great sales force can be beaten down by a bad economy, a new competitor, or even a nasty rumor in the marketplace. So what should be the objective criteria for "good"?

Of course, sales forces have to be judged ultimately by their performance against Business Results, like making quota. But Revenue is too blunt a measure to reveal definitively whether or not a sales force is any good. That's where Sales Objectives can help. Sales Objectives put a more sophisticated lens on a sales force's performance and give us greater confidence that leadership has built a good sales force.

If a sales force is the right size to execute its go-to-market strategy, is consistently increasing its selling capability, is capturing the right customers, and is selling the right products, then you *have* to say that it's a good sales force. What more could you ask? If the Business Results aren't coming, then either expectations were set too high, or there is something else working against the sales force. It's still a good sales force because it's achieving all of its Sales Objectives.

In our opinion, Sales Objectives should not only be the key performance metrics for a sales force but also the indicators of good sales management. If the Sales Objectives are set properly and the sales force is meeting them, then it's a gold star for sales leadership. Conversely, if the Business Results *are* being met but the sales force is mangling the Sales Objectives, then management gets a silver star, at best.

This last point begs another fundamental question:

What is the role of a sales force?

If its role is to simply churn out acceptable Business Results quarter after quarter, then a sales force can absolutely succeed with brute force and dumb luck. And there are many organizations that are content with this role. How often do we hear marketing complain that its sales force isn't executing the company's product or customer strategy only to hear sales respond, "Well, we hit our numbers." We hear it a lot. In companies like these, the Sales Objectives are totally irrelevant when compared to good Business Results.

However, there are many organizations that do *not* find it acceptable to make the numbers by any means possible. These companies view their sales forces as strategic weapons against the competition. With capable salespeople who can be directed toward specific customers with specific products, they are market leaders that can nimbly shift gears to take advantage of new buying trends or strategic opportunities. Of course these sales forces also have to achieve their Business Results, but they do so in a disciplined and controlled manner.

This is why Sales Objectives are so vitally important. They give management a deeper level of control over the performance of its sales force: "Don't just bring us revenue—bring us the right revenue in the right way. And here is what we mean by right." When desired Business Results are supported with relevant Sales Objectives, the sales management code begins to crack a little more.

STATUS CHECK

As we dug yet deeper into our unfolding management framework, we examined the Sales Objectives that lie in between the highly manageable Sales Activities and the totally unmanageable Business Results. We found that there are four distinct Sales Objectives that provide guidance and diagnoses that are specifically useful to sales management:

1. **Market Coverage**, which measures whether the sales force has enough selling capacity to pursue all of its desired opportunities in the marketplace
2. **Sales Force Capability**, which reveals whether the salespeople and managers are skilled and enabled to effectively execute their Sales Activities
3. **Customer Focus**, which indicates whether the sales force is successfully capturing the company's desired types of customers
4. **Product Focus**, which informs whether the sales force is successfully selling the company's preferred products and services

If all of these objectives are met, then you will have an amply sized sales force that is willing and able to execute your company's stated

SALES OBJECTIVE	PURPOSE OF METRICS	SAMPLE METRICS IN STUDY
Market Coverage	Ensure there is enough total selling effort to engage all desired customers and prospects	• # of Total Selling Hours • % of Customers Called • % Customer-Facing Time
Sales Force Capability	Ensure that salespeople are using their capacity effectively during their individual customer interactions	• Win/Loss Ratio • % of Deals Advancing by Stage • Length of Sales Cycle
Customer Focus	Ensure the sales force is capturing, retaining, and growing the customers that the company wants to have	• # of New Accounts • % Customer Retention • % Share of Wallet
Product Focus	Ensure the sales force is selling the products and service that the company wants to sell	• Revenue by Product • Cross-Sell Rate • Average Deal Size

FIGURE 4.7

Sales Objectives with Corresponding Metrics

go-to-market strategy. In our opinion, you will have a great sales force. See Figure 4.7.

Beyond being "great," your sales force will be more under your control than a sales force that is left to find its own path to your targeted Business Results. In the absence of clear Sales Objectives, sales managers and salespeople will do what they think is best. But their individual assumptions could leave you with an inefficient, ineffective sales force that sells the wrong products to the wrong customers.

If your organization is indifferent to how your Business Results are achieved (and many companies are), then it can also be indifferent to the setting of Sales Objectives. However, if it wants a sales force that is a genuine competitive advantage, then Sales Objectives are a critical management tool. They allow leadership to shift go-to-market strategies as business conditions dictate while knowing with confidence that its sales force will react accordingly. Crisp Sales Objectives are the difference between a chaotic selling effort and a precision selling effort. For any organization that offers an assortment of products to a diverse customer base, a laissez-faire management strategy is a high-risk and potentially wasteful approach.

So as we continued our quest for the operating instructions to the sales force, we were pleased to find these Sales Objectives conveniently nestled between Business Results and Sales Activities. They provide much-needed guideposts for sales management to steer field-level activity toward executive-level expectations. If the sales manager is the most critical link in the chain of command from the war room to the battlefield, then Sales Objectives are the marching orders. Without them, the fight might get ugly. With them, the execution of the battle plan can be flawless.

Marching orders in hand, we now turned our attention to deciphering the most tactical portion of the sales management code: Sales Activities.

Sales Activities— the Drivers of Sales Performance

CHAPTER 5

THE MISSING METRICS ON THE WALL

As the 306 metrics slowly found their rightful places on our own war room wall, we were eventually left with only the numbers that can truly be managed. Of course, these were measures of Sales Activities. Compared to Business Results or Sales Objectives, these metrics are extremely cooperative because they measure the things that a sales force actually does. Pursuing leads, planning for sales calls, visiting prospects, strategizing opportunities, and managing customer relationships are the day-to-day activities that are done in pursuit of Sales Objectives and Business Results. Perform these tasks efficiently and effectively, and achieving your quota is a breeze. Fumble around and misplace your effort, and any goal feels like a stretch. Plainly stated, these things are important.

Imagine our disappointment, then, to find that more than 80% of our 306 numbers were already pinned to other walls. That means that only 17% of the metrics in our study were intended to measure the Sales Activities that actually determine sales success or failure. So while these activities are critically important to every organization, it appears that measuring the quality and quantity of them is not.

Let us reiterate that these are all of the things that a sales force actually does. No one "does" revenue or product mix, but everyone makes sales calls. *All* of what the sales force does resides in this bucket, yet more than 80% of what management chooses to measure resides elsewhere. Hmm. If a goal of management is to gain greater control over sales force behaviors, then it would seem we had uncovered a very large problem.

You've probably heard the old management adage that "what gets measured gets done." Ironically, it appears that in most sales forces, what gets done doesn't get measured. As you might expect, we've questioned many sales leaders over the years on why this is the case, and there are two primary reasons that they typically offer in response. One concerns their ability to collect credible data, and another regards their desire to use it. While we can appreciate their objections, we find that they both are fading in relevance.

The first objection we encounter when we push clients to report more Sales Activity metrics is that activity-level data is difficult to collect, and this is somewhat true. While information such as a customer's purchasing history can be easily extracted from a company's financial reporting system, information about a sales rep's activities typically cannot. Capturing this type of data often requires some manual intervention, including the need for reps to enter information themselves.

Not only do many managers not want their reps spending time on data entry, nearly as many will tell you that they don't trust the information that their sales reps provide. To us, these arguments are remnants of a bygone era when information technology was not pervasive and salespeople were lone rangers. When we hear sales reps ask, "Would you rather me be in front of a computer or in front of a customer?" we respond, "Both." And when we hear a manager say, "My reps just lie about their call volumes when they put them into the system," we say, "Then fire them." In the twenty-first century, people interact with electronic devices constantly, and salespeople are expected to be professionals. If management wants activity-level data to help it manage its sales force, then it needs to set the expectation and then make it happen. We work with many organizations where this is the case, and they have better managers because of it.

The second objection that we often hear is that managers don't even want activity-level data on their salespeople. Here, the argument goes that they don't wish to give the appearance of micromanaging their sellers. A curious instance of this sentiment occurred several years ago when we were researching the sales management practices of several top sales forces in the United States.[1] One head of sales explained to us quite apologetically that his company regretfully collected and reported activity-level metrics. He confided, "Yeah, we do collect a lot of data on our salespeople's activities. I guess we're just kind of old-school in that way."

We would contend that collecting activity-level metrics is not old-school whatsoever—we think it is *new* school. And we would argue that tracking salespeople's activities won't lead to micromanagement—it will lead to *proactive* management. Technology has enabled us to collect these metrics in less intrusive ways, and our new sales management framework will enable us to use the data in a more sophisticated manner. Going forward, we hope that all war room walls will have a fair representation of Sales Activity metrics, since managing those numbers is what aligns sales force behaviors with desired outcomes. Whether old or new, that's the school for us.

SALES PROCESSES, YOU SAY?

Clearly we believe that measuring Sales Activities is a key ingredient to better sales management. However, reporting data on salespeople's doings is not sufficient to exercise control over a sales force's performance. To truly exert influence over Sales Objectives and Business Results, sales managers must not only

---

1. Our "World Class Sales Excellence Research Report" may be downloaded at http://www.vantagepointperformance.com.

receive relevant data, they must know what to do with it. They therefore need a way to organize a sales force's activities into a coherent operating system with predictable inputs and outputs. They need a set of formal business processes.

As we discussed earlier in this book, other business functions like manufacturing or finance are typically managed with a higher level of rigor than the sales force. In large part, this is because other corporate functions have formal business processes in place that allow for consistent execution and robust measurement of their daily activities. This visibility into the gears and pulleys of a workforce is required in order to exercise control and continuously improve. In the absence of standardized processes to enable active management, sales leadership often finds itself in the war room attempting to herd cats rather than direct soldiers. Sales managers have unmanageable chaos rather than command over their troops.

This point was colorfully illustrated by a conversation we once had with a senior executive of a $400 million software company whose revenues had stalled. He was frustrated by his company's inability to improve its sales force's productivity, so he approached us for advice. Our initial conversation contained an exchange that went something like this:

> **Vantage Point Performance:** *So you have a little more than 250 salespeople in the field?*
>
> **Discouraged Senior Executive:** *That's right.*
>
> **VPP:** *And what exactly do they do?*
>
> **Executive:** *They find new customers for our software.*
>
> **VPP:** *How do they find new customers?*
>
> **Executive:** *You know. They prospect in their territories and then try to close whatever deals that they uncover.*
>
> **VPP:** *And how do they do that? I'm trying to understand the processes they follow, so I can get a better sense of where the problem might be.*
>
> **Executive:** *I don't know what processes they follow—you'd have to ask them.*
>
> **VPP:** *You don't have any kind of standard sales processes for your sales force to follow?*

Executive: *No. It's up to the salespeople to find new business any way they can. That's their job.*

(Pause)

VPP: *So you have 250 people in the field selling in potentially 250 different ways?*

Executive: *Potentially, yes.*

VPP: *How different are the customers they sell to? Do they all buy from you in a similar way?*

Executive: *Sure. Given the technical nature of our products, we end up selling to pretty much the same type of customer. Their buying patterns are probably very similar.*

VPP: *So do you think there might be a "best" way to go about selling to those customers?*

Executive: *I'm sure there is, but I don't know what it would be. That's why we have the sales force . . . to figure that out.*

VPP: *Well, OK, but if you have no standard sales process, then how can you measure how successful your salespeople are at doing whatever it is that they do?*

Executive: *Well, of course, we know how much they each sell. But that's about it.*

VPP: *How long is the average sales cycle?*

Executive: *Around six months or so, on average.*

VPP: *And you don't measure anything that they do for the six months leading up to a sale?*

Executive: *No, not that I'm aware of.*

(Longer pause)

VPP: *So, you have 250 salespeople, with no formal sales process, doing something (you don't know what) to your customers over a six-month period, and you have no metrics to track and improve the effectiveness of their selling activities?*

Executive: *That pretty much sums it up. I'm sensing from your question that you think that's a problem?*

VPP: *Well, if your burning issue is an inability to proactively improve your sales force's performance, I'd say that is the problem.*

Executive: *Hmm. I've never really thought of it that way. You're probably onto something, though.*

Like many, this senior executive knew very little about what his sales force actually did from day to day. His VP of sales had to-date employed the management-by-results approach of offering his sales reps very high commissions and then "getting out of the way to let them do their job." Unfortunately, that strategy backfired when revenue growth slowed. Without formal sales processes and measurements in place, he had little visibility into his sales force's activities and even less control over them. It is a very frustrating place for an executive to be.

This conversation took place many years ago, and most sales leaders today know that formal sales processes are required for effective management. However, the term *sales process* is still a very murky concept for most. During our careers, we have heard the term *sales process* used in as many different ways as one can imagine. And that single fact points to a fundamental challenge of controlling sales performance: *we don't have a common framework or a common language to manage the Sales Activities that drive sales performance.* We need a better understanding of the fundamental business processes that are at work within every sales force.

It's worth noting that several people advised us during the writing of this book *not* to use the term *sales process.* They warned that *process* is a dangerous word that could confuse readers, since each company defines its sales processes in its own way. And that is the precise reason that this book is needed. Every sales force should *customize* its sales processes to the way it does business, but it should not be responsible for *defining* what sales processes are. There should be a common discipline within the field of sales for how things work. Further, that discipline should be taught to sales managers just like generally accepted accounting principles are taught to accountants and total quality management is taught to engineers. Without it, sales managers are forced to make it up as they go along. Every single time.

Therefore, we felt that to truly crack the sales management code, we had to wrestle this issue to the ground. It was not enough to merely identify that Sales Activities are the most basic levers for controlling a sales force—we had to discover how those levers fit into manageable sales processes. We had to figure out how sales managers could organize and direct their sales-people's activities to predictably influence all the other metrics on the wall. If we could do that, we would have done something meaningful. If not, the sales force would remain a collection of seemingly unrelated activities, and the chaos would persist.

THE BUILDING BLOCKS OF CONTROL

We braced ourselves for the expectedly arduous task of definitively identifying the fundamental processes at work in every sales force. Given the fact that it had never been done before, we assumed that we would struggle mightily to tease out distinct sales processes that would encompass all of the remaining metrics on our wall. Surprisingly, the task proved to be quite easy.

Each of these remaining metrics was collected by sales management to make sure that some type of selling activity was taking place. And if the activities were important enough to measure, then each of them most certainly pointed toward the achievement of a very specific goal. Therefore, to identify the nature of each specific sales process, we simply had to determine the desired outcome of each activity. Within minutes, we had shuffled the remaining numbers on our wall into five separate processes—four for the sales rep's activities and one for sales management's (see Figure 5.1). We had extracted from the metrics the fundamental building blocks for gaining control over a sales force. The code had finally cracked, and we were on the cusp of mapping once and for all the sales force's DNA.

First, we found measures of activity that were directed toward effective Call Management. These metrics, such as Percentage of Reps Doing Call Planning and Call Plan Usage, are intended to ensure that sales calls or meetings are conducted effectively. In our study, navigating an individual sales call was the most elemental form of sales process.

If you string together several sales calls in pursuit of a single deal, then you will need to employ the second type of sales

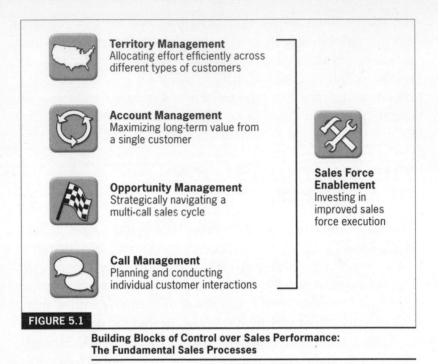

FIGURE 5.1

**Building Blocks of Control over Sales Performance:
The Fundamental Sales Processes**

process we observed, Opportunity Management. Metrics that measure Opportunity Management, such as Opportunity Plan Usage or Adherence to Opportunity Planning Process, make certain that salespeople are thoughtfully pursuing individual deals.

If you find that you are pursuing multiple deals over time with a single customer, then you might choose to engage in our third sales process, Account Management. Account Management metrics such as Percentage of Account Plans Complete or Number of Interactions per Account measure the sales rep's effort in retaining and growing existing customer relationships.

And finally for the salesperson, if you target many customers and have to allocate your time efficiently across them, then you are engaging in Territory Management. Measures such as Number of Calls Made or Number of Meetings per Customer Type track sellers' efforts to call on the right customers in the right quantity.

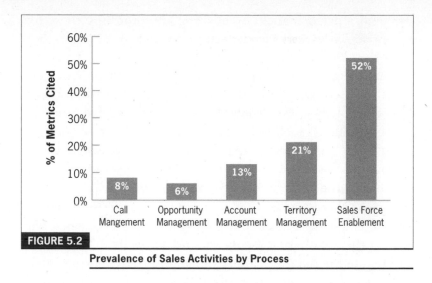

FIGURE 5.2

Prevalence of Sales Activities by Process

We also found several types of metrics that were used to gauge how well sales management is preparing its sales force to succeed. We called them collectively the Sales Force Enablement process, and they include numbers such as Percentage of Time Spent Coaching and Training Investment per FTE.[2] These varied measures help to focus sales management on developing and supporting the capabilities of its sellers. Sales Force Enablement metrics were by far the most common Sales Activity measure found in our study (see Figure 5.2).

Remarkably, all of the Sales Activity metrics on our wall fell neatly into one of these five sales processes. When we stepped back and looked at the categories we had formed, we marveled at the simplicity. These truly are the most fundamental things that a salesperson does: make sales calls to win opportunities to gain customers within their territories. And sales managers enable those efforts by equipping and developing their sellers. That's it, the skeleton of a sales force. A marvel of simplicity.

Sure, there's plenty of other stuff going on in the sales force, but these are the fundamentals, the basic processes that

---

2. FTE is the acronym for a full-time equivalent employee: two full-time workers = two FTEs, while two half-time workers = one FTE.

drive sales performance. By pushing and prodding these five sets of activities, sales leaders can influence all of the higher-level metrics in our sales management framework. These are the numbers that can be changed at will by sales managers, and doing so gives them the power to accomplish any Sales Objective or Business Result they desire. These five processes are the building blocks of control over a sales force.

Just like "discovering" that you can't manage revenue, this discovery was a bit of a brick-meet-forehead moment. *Of course* this is what the sales force is trying to do. *Of course* these are the things we should measure if we want to proactively manage a sales force's performance. But then again, if it's so obvious, why weren't there more of these metrics on our wall?

Despite the relative scarcity of Sales Activity metrics in our study, these five processes are the levers and pulleys that control a sales force. They are essential mechanisms of sales management. So we will spend a good deal of time exploring the five processes that encompass our Sales Activities. We will also share observations on the metrics, tools, and common issues that typically relate to each.

To sales force generals, this chapter might seem a little like boot camp. These are the fundamentals of hand-to-hand combat, and any experienced salesperson has participated in all of these processes to some degree. However, gaining a crisp and comprehensive understanding of each will enable you to direct the battles on the field with greater insight and impact. After we detail these final pieces of sales management code, we will explore how to assemble a unique management system to decorate your own war room walls.

Call Management

No doubt, making sales calls is the most essential task of the salesperson. Whether face-to-face, over the telephone, or even through some electronic means, direct interactions between a seller and a buyer are at the core of every salesperson's role. For that matter, they are the very reason that a company needs a sales force. If an organization made no sales calls, it would need no salespeople. So if a company has a sales force, you can bet it's making calls.

The nature of a sales call can vary greatly, though, ranging from an inbound phone call to an off-site customer retreat. The frequency of sales calls can also vary wildly—a retail sales rep may participate in dozens of "calls" each day, while a strategic account manager may only make a dozen face-to-face sales calls in a year. Regardless of the nature or frequency, the quality of the seller-buyer interaction will determine whether or not a sale is made. Do the right things during a sales call, and the sale will move forward. Do the wrong things, and the sale will come to an abrupt and unwelcomed end. Therefore, companies often engage in activities to improve the quality of their sales calls. These activities comprise a Call Management process.

The Activities. Call Management is a vital process for many salespeople. Of course, managing a sales call really comes down to careful planning, execution, and reflection on the part of the seller, and sales managers can play a very valuable role in helping their salespeople navigate these elemental sales activities. Unfortunately, managers cannot manage the *outcomes* of a call— successful call outcomes are Sales Objectives, since they require agreement from the buyer. But a sales manager can heavily influence the outcomes of sales calls by guiding the salesperson through the process.

Foremost in the process, sales reps must *prepare for the call*. A thorough call-planning exercise forces salespeople to set clear objectives for the call, plan what they intend to do, anticipate what the buyer might do in response, and identify alternative actions in case things deviate from the plan. This straightforward activity can have a dramatic impact on the quality of the sales call and the likelihood of a successful outcome.

Second, salespeople must *execute the call*. This is the main event of selling. While there are many factors that affect the ultimate outcome of a sale, nothing is more significant than a seller's direct interactions with the buyer. This is the salesperson's best chance to uncover key information and to influence the buyer's thinking in a robust, iterative dialogue. During

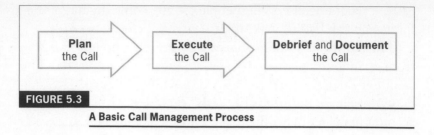

Plan the Call → Execute the Call → Debrief and Document the Call

FIGURE 5.3

A Basic Call Management Process

every call, a seller can dramatically improve or decrease her likelihood of winning the deal. This is why thorough call preparation is so very important. You've got to know you're doing. See Figure 5.3.

This brings us to the final Call Management activity, which is to *debrief the call*. During a post-call debriefing session, the sales manager and rep document the call outcomes and discuss the good, bad, and ugly of what took place. Whether or not he accompanied his salesperson on the call, the manager should help the seller reflect on her own performance and critically evaluate her decisions and actions. A call debrief can be one of the most powerful developmental activities for a salesperson, particularly under the guidance of a skilled coach.

The Metrics. Most of the Call Management metrics we observed were focused on pre-call planning activities. Commonly, these are measures that track whether salespeople are adhering to a call planning methodology or using their call planning tools. In our study, we observed a handful of these measures, like Adherence to Call Planning Process and Call Plan Usage (see Figure 5.4). These metrics can be collected in a variety of ways, including sales force surveys, sales manager observations, and reports that are generated from the planning tools themselves.

It is possible to track performance in the other stages of the Call Management process, too. In-call metrics might include Number of Questions Asked, Sales Rep Talk Time, or other measures of salesperson behavior during the call. Metrics such as these are best obtained by observing sales reps in action, and

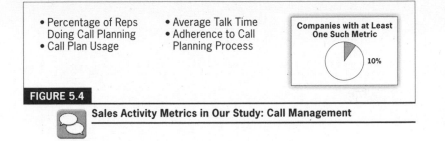

they can provide great insights into the skills and practices of a seller.

Metrics can also be reported on post-call activities such as coaching and completing documentation. Measures like Percentage of Calls with Debrief or Number of Calls Logged in CRM can ensure that these important tasks are occurring. Again, manual intervention is required to capture these numbers, but if Call Management is a critical activity for your sales force, then it is worth the investment of time to know that you're maximizing the value of each and every sales call.

The Tools. The primary tool to support Call Management is, of course, the call plan. Call plans take salespeople through a structured and thorough approach to preparing for an upcoming sales call (see Figure 5.5). Call plans help reps conduct an effective customer interaction by forcing them to consider questions like these:

- What are the call objectives?
- What are the customer's likely needs?
- What information does the seller want to learn?
- What questions should the seller ask?
- Which products or services should the seller and the customer discuss?
- What objections might arise?

Increasingly, call plans are integrated into a company's CRM tool, though they can be just as effective on paper or in a desktop publishing application. We find that too often people obsess

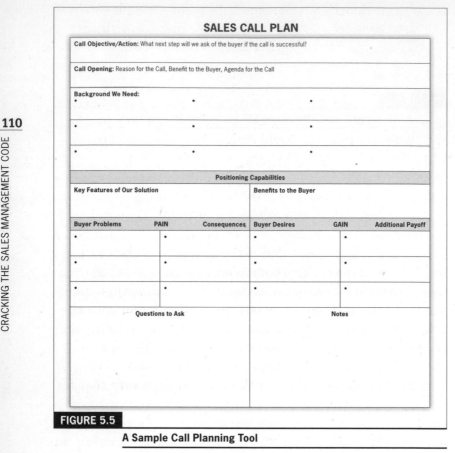

SALES CALL PLAN

Call Objective/Action: What next step will we ask of the buyer if the call is successful?

Call Opening: Reason for the Call, Benefit to the Buyer, Agenda for the Call

Background We Need:

Positioning Capabilities	
Key Features of Our Solution	**Benefits to the Buyer**

Buyer Problems	PAIN	Consequences	Buyer Desires	GAIN	Additional Payoff

Questions to Ask	Notes

FIGURE 5.5

A Sample Call Planning Tool

over the format or medium for their sales force's call plans. The truth is, the point of call planning is not to create a plan. The only reason to create a call plan is to ensure that the planning took place. You simply want to make certain that the salesperson thoughtfully prepared for the call before it took place. Simply stated: the plan means nothing, but the plann*ing* means everything.

Common Issues. The most common question we get when working with clients to implement call planning processes, tools, and metrics is, When should a salesperson take the time to plan a sales call? Our first reaction is that a seller should *never* call on a customer without some level of forethought—even if it's just to consider why the salesperson is there, why the buyer should care, and what the seller hopes to accomplish.

However, *formal* call planning is much more time-intensive than just considering a few basic questions. Depending on the volume of calls a salesperson makes, it's often impractical for him to formally plan every call he makes on every prospect or customer. Doing so could consume days out of his week. Therefore, we tell our clients this:

> **Formal call planning should be done only when it is needed.**

Our advice is to use a call planning process when a call is particularly important or somehow high-risk. Many routine sales calls don't warrant the extra effort that formal planning requires, and forcing reps to complete a plan when it's a low-value exercise transforms planning into administration. Sales managers need to set expectations with their salespeople as to when and how call planning should take place. Then, of course, they should measure the process to ensure that it's happening.

A second issue that we often need to address with clients surrounds who is involved in the call planning process.

> **Call planning should involve both the salesperson *and* his manager.**

Too often, call planning is considered the salesperson's sole responsibility, and his manager's only involvement is enforcing compliance with the process. "Did you do a call plan?" "Yep." "Great." While this is efficient for the manager, it misses two opportunities to leverage the Call Management process into higher performance and improved capability.

First, when managers work *with* their salespeople to develop call plans, the quality of the plan is almost always better. Beyond the fact that "two heads are better than one," the manager's own selling experience can help the seller identify holes in his preparation or flaws in his reasoning. Improved call outcomes result from a collaborative planning effort.

Second, the call planning process is a perfect opportunity for developmental coaching. It provides a structured and safe environment for a manager to assess his salespeople's critical thinking skills and coach them to increased capability. Over time, collaborative planning not only leads to better calls, it leads to a better sales force.

In summary, Call Management is one of the most elemental ways that sales managers can exert control over the performance of their salespeople. By influencing the quality and the content of their sales force's calls, managers can achieve specific Sales Objectives by guiding the behaviors of their reps in the field. In the absence of deliberate Call Management, sales reps will make critical decisions in the midst of battle. With a formal Call Management process, the battle plans will be drawn with a little more care.

Opportunity Management

Most sales are not completed in a single customer interaction and require many sales calls before the sale is finally closed. Sales that involve multiple calls across different stages of a customer's buying process might require an additional layer of sales process to navigate the opportunity successfully. In addition to managing the individual sales calls, it's wise for salespeople to think deliberately about how they approach the end-to-end selling effort. This process is called Opportunity Management.

The Activities. Opportunity Management is a group of activities that helps a seller examine, qualify, strategize, and execute a single multistage sales pursuit. Like Call Management, there are both conceptual and tactical elements to Opportunity Management. But unlike managing individual calls, managing opportunities requires wider and longer-range vision, since there are more moving parts to consider in a complex sales cycle.

First the salesperson must *gather information* that is needed to fully assess the opportunity in the context of the customer, the seller's organization, the competition, and other environmental factors. This information can come from online services, conversations with the customer, annual reports, records of previous customer interactions, industry publications, marketplace gossip, and just about any other source of information that one can imagine. Until full information is known about the opportunity and its surrounding circumstances, good planning cannot take place.

Once sufficient information has been gathered, the seller must *qualify the opportunity* to ensure that it's worth pursuit. This should be done by judging the opportunity against clearly defined criteria that will steer your sales force toward deals that align with your company's go-to-market strategy. If formal criteria *are* in place, your sales force will become expert collectors of highly desirable leads. If formal criteria are not in place, your salespeople will spin their wheels pursuing unwinnable or undesirable deals. Many sellers struggle to disqualify bad opportunities, and it shows in the bleak percentage of deals that actually win.

Next the salesperson must *form a strategy* to shepherd the opportunity successfully from beginning to end. This involves deciding how to align her company's selling activities with the different stages and different participants in the customer's buying process. Additionally, the seller has to determine how to best position her company's products or services against those of the competition. With a coherent strategy in place, the salesperson can close a deal efficiently and effectively. Without a coherent plan, the seller can resemble a pinball being bounced around by every unanticipated discovery. No one wants to be a pinball.

Of course, your organization must then *execute the strategy* according to the plan. We say that your entire organization must execute because resources from anywhere inside a company can be engaged in an opportunity pursuit. In addition to the salesperson, there might be resources from engineering, marketing, finance, or other departments carrying out tasks

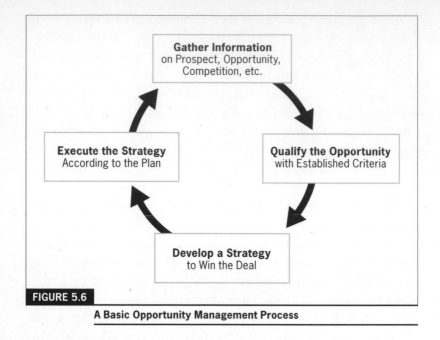

FIGURE 5.6

A Basic Opportunity Management Process

in an opportunity plan. Even external resources such as other customers or industry luminaries are frequently involved in winning a complex opportunity. As with all winning strategies, accurate execution is crucial.

Unlike a Call Management process that has a discrete beginning and end, Opportunity Management is a circular process (see Figure 5.6). Once an organization begins to execute its plan, more information will come to light that could require a course correction in the strategy or even disqualify the opportunity altogether. Opportunity Management is iterative and should be expected to evolve as the sale progresses. Round and round the process goes, until someone makes a sale.

The Metrics. As with Call Management, the Opportunity Management metrics on our wall were mostly intended to measure compliance with the process. These were measures like Number of Opportunity Plans Completed or Adherence to Opportunity Planning Process. Also like Call Management, these metrics can be collected through sales force surveys, sales

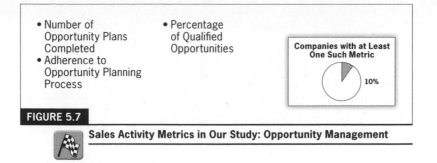

FIGURE 5.7

115

Sales Activity Metrics in Our Study: Opportunity Management

manager observations, or reports that are generated from the Opportunity Management tools themselves.

Disappointingly, *very* few companies in our study collected metrics on the activities associated with Opportunity Management (see Figure 5.7). However, the variety of metrics that could be reported is only limited by the nature of your sales process. One company in our research did track the percentage of opportunities that had been qualified by the sales force. We've known other sales forces that chose to measure things like the number of opportunities during which engineers, executives, or other company personnel accompanied their frontline sellers on sales calls because they felt it increased their chances of winning deals. We've also seen sales forces track the number of times certain products were proposed or certain types of buyers were contacted in an effort to shift focus among different products or customers. If it's an important activity in pursuit of an opportunity, it can be tracked and reported in some fashion.

The Tools. The primary tool to support the Opportunity Management process is the opportunity plan. The format and contents of an opportunity plan should be customized to fit the way your sales force sells, but it is commonly designed to help salespeople thoughtfully answer opportunity-related questions like these:

- What is the nature of the opportunity?
- Is the opportunity qualified?
- Who are the participants in the buying process?

- What is important to them?
- Who is the competition?
- What are our competitive strengths and weaknesses?
- What will we offer the customers and why?
- What must we do to win?
- What are the steps in the sale?
- Who should be involved in the sales process?
- Where are their responsibilities?

Like any planning tool, opportunity plans encourage structured thinking and make certain that all angles have been considered (see Figure 5.8). They can also serve as project plans for a deal pursuit team to organize its activities and track their completion. And of course, opportunity planning sessions provide an excellent venue for sales managers to coach their reps. When done collaboratively, the quality and impact of opportunity planning is greatly increased.

Other Opportunity Management tools are those that assist a seller in doing background research. During an opportunity pursuit, much information is needed as inputs to the process— information on the industry, company, buyers, competitors, marketplace, and so on. Useful tools for doing such research include external sources like online information services or networking tools, as well as internal sources like company intranets, CRM applications, or financial systems. Accurate and ample information enables good decision-making throughout the Opportunity Management process.

Common Issues. For a moment we'll overlook the glaringly obvious issue that Opportunity Management, like Call Management, is being measured by so few companies. (Though it's mind-boggling to consider that every sales force in the world makes sales calls and most pursue multistage deals, *but* these make-or-break activities are largely being left to chance in the field.) Instead, we'll focus on the ironic fact that many leadership teams stand in their war rooms staring at shriveling pipelines, but their walls are missing the data that would help them drive pipeline growth. This is why:

> **Opportunity and Call Management are the processes used to manage a sales pipeline.**

And as we mentioned before, we had loads of "Sales Pipeline" numbers on our wall before we recategorized them as Business Results or Sales Objectives. These metrics chronicled in great detail the size of a pipeline, the shape of a pipeline, and how capable a sales force is at moving deals through it. However, there were no pipeline numbers that got shuttled to the Sales Activity space.

That's because there is no distinct pipeline management process. The sales pipeline is actually aggregated data on a sales force's opportunities and calls. Milestones along a sales

SALES OPPORTUNITY PLAN

Company:	
Opportunity:	
Team Leader:	
Last Update:	

Qualification

Defined Need:	Winnable?
Approved Budget:	Timeline to Purchase:

Buyers

Name	Type	Needs	Level of Support

Competition

Company	Strengths	Weaknesses

Strategy

Offering	Value Proposition	Positioning

Next Steps

Objective	Person Responsible	Action Item/Completion Date

Stage

Level	Qualified	Demo	Proposal	Negotiate	Win/Loss

FIGURE 5.8

A Sample Opportunity Planning Tool

opportunity are the backbone of a pipeline, and successful sales calls are how opportunities advance through the sales cycle. *Therefore, the closest you can get to managing your sales pipeline is to manage your salespeople's opportunities and calls.*

In short, Opportunity Management and Call Management *are* pipeline management, and the only way to proactively improve your pipeline is to formalize these two processes and track their associated metrics. Otherwise, your pipeline management processes will remain ad hoc in nature and, even worse, invisible to you. These numbers should be on war room walls, right beside the higher-level pipeline metrics that many executives can't live without.

A second issue we observe regarding Opportunity Management is a tendency to develop opportunity plans that are far too complex. The goal of an opportunity plan is to ensure that structured thinking and planning is taking place on importing deals.

> **The goal is *not* to document all possible information about an opportunity.**

We often see companies treat opportunity plans as a comprehensive database of information on every aspect of an opportunity. The plan can be pages long and include data so tangential to the core opportunity that it looks more like a corporate biography than a plan to pursue a single deal. Leadership is prone to defend such monumental documents by saying, "If this salesperson died tomorrow, I'd want anyone in the sales force to be able to pick up this plan and finish the deal." Interesting.

While it's exceedingly unlikely that salespeople will start dropping dead en masse, we do understand management's craving for visibility into important opportunities. The challenge is this: the more burdensome planning becomes, the less compliant sales reps will be to the process. Our advice is to keep Opportunity Management activities as streamlined as possible and focused on the task of enabling better selling. A greater level of process and rigor will almost always elevate salespeople's performance, but too much rigor can kill them. Remember: the plan means nothing—the plan*ing* means everything.

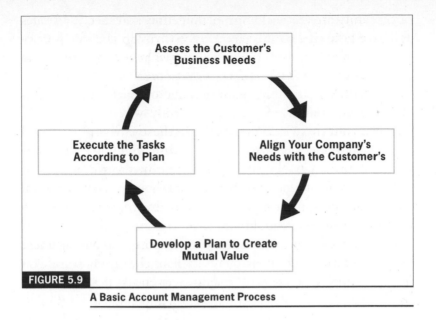

FIGURE 5.9

A Basic Account Management Process

Account Management

If Peter Drucker was correct that the most basic purpose of a business is to create a customer, then there is a higher purpose that he forgot to mention: to create a *repeat* customer. Customers who purchase from you repeatedly over time not only provide an ongoing stream of revenue, but the cost of sale to existing customers is often substantially lower than that of faceless prospects. Any way you look at it, repeat customers fall squarely into the category of Things a Company Wants to Have.

If your company receives a high proportion of its revenues from a concentrated number of loyal customers, then you need to be very deliberate about how you handle those critical relationships. There is a particular set of activities that can prove very useful in helping your organization retain and grow those existing relationships. Collectively, they're known as an Account Management process (see Figure 5.9).

The Activities. The ultimate goal of Account Management is to maximize the long-term value of a select group of customers. Whether these customers are the biggest, most profitable, or otherwise strategically important, they warrant additional attention from the seller's company in order to increase loyalty and profits. Account Management activities essentially tailor a company's go-to-market strategy to each chosen customer through careful analysis, planning, and execution at the individual account level.

The first activity in a good Account Management process is to *assess your customer's business needs.* By understanding your customer's long-range strategy and short-term objectives, you can not only align your products and services with its top-of-mind issues, you can also look for innovative ways to help your customer further its own business objectives. Research shows that customers highly value suppliers that have an innovative eye and proactively bring new ideas to their customers.[3] This can only happen if you invest the time to assess your customer's business deeply.

Once the customer's needs are known, you must develop an account strategy that will *align your company's needs with the needs of your customer.* Clearly your company will have its own agenda for the account—increasing Share of Wallet, introducing a new product line, expanding into other parts of its organization, or some other Sales Objective that will yield better Business Results. However, your agenda can only be accomplished if it in some way supports the customer's agenda. A winning account strategy will consider both sides of the relationship and find strategic alignment between your organizations' goals.

Of course, that winning strategy can only be brought to life if you *develop a plan* outlining the required tasks. The planning effort should be led by the salesperson, but it could include people from across the seller's organization. In addition to the salesperson's manager, account planning often engages other sellers who assist with cross-selling, operational staff who improve customer service levels, external partners who provide related services, executives who engage the customer at higher levels, or any other people who must play a role in achieving your goals for the account.

3. Howard Stevens and Theodore Kinni, *Achieve Sales Excellence* (Avon, MA: Platinum Press, 2007).

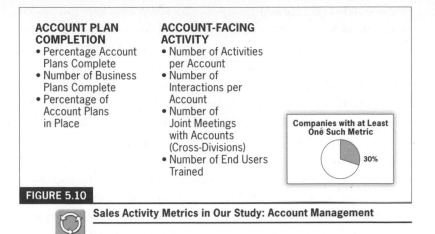

FIGURE 5.10

Sales Activity Metrics in Our Study: Account Management

Finally, there's the pesky chore of flawlessly executing the plan. Account Management is very much a team sport, and in this case, the salesperson is the coach. Not only must your seller diagram the plays in the account plan, she must ensure that her teammates are performing as expected. It can be challenging for a salesperson to coordinate resources that are not accountable to her, but the seller must find a way to rally the necessary troops. It's the salesperson who is ultimately accountable to her customer . . . and to her manager . . . and to her quota. So she is the one who has to make it happen.

The Metrics. The Account Management metrics we saw on our wall fell into one of two categories. Like Call Management and Opportunity Management, there were numbers that were intended to drive compliance with the planning process. In the case of Account Management, all of these metrics assured that plann*ing* was taking place by assuring that the *plans* were in place. Measures like Percentage of Account Plans in Place or Number of Business Plans Completed were reported, as you might expect.

The second group of numbers was focused on tracking interactions between the company and its customers (see Figure 5.10). Metrics like Number of Activities per Account and Number of Joint Meetings with Accounts reveal not only the intensity of customer relationships but also the nature of their interactions. Depending on your go-to-market strategy or the contents of your account plans, you could track a metric for nearly any customer-facing activity.

The Tools. As you can see from the first group of metrics, an account plan is the key tool for Account Management activities. Account plans can range in size from a page to a small book, depending on the level of detail that an account plan captures. Regardless of the plan's size, the tools are used to take a salesperson or the account team through a structured process of setting account objectives and planning how to achieve them. Questions that are commonly asked include these:

- What are the customer's strategic initiatives?
- How can we help the customer accomplish them?
- What do we want to get from this account?
- What will we have to give them to get it?
- Who are the key stakeholders at the account?
- Do they consider us friend or foe?
- What do we need to do in the next month, quarter, year, or longer?
- Who from our organization must be involved?
- What must they specifically do and when?

The list of potential questions could literally go on forever. Account plans can include information such as customer financial data, past purchasing history, incumbent competitors, issues between the two organizations, industry dynamics, and anything else that the seller's company thinks is important or somehow interesting (see Figure 5.11). Practically, the length to which account plans can go is sometimes limited by the number of accounts the organization deems plan-worthy. If each salesperson is planning for 20 customers, then clearly the account plans must be rudimentary. However, if 20 people inside the selling organization are dedicated to a single large account, then it might require a book-sized document to hold information required for each of the many stakeholders.

KEY ACCOUNT PLAN

Last Update:

General Information	Primary Customer Contacts
Customer Name: Account Leader:	Key Contact Function Relationship

What We Want	What They Want
This Year Next Year Revenue: Gross Margin: Share of Wallet: Installed Products: Strategic Objectives:	Timeline to Purchase: Stated Needs: Latent Needs: Issues to Resolve:

Action Plan

Action Items	Owner	Completion Date
1. _____		
2. _____		
3. _____		
4. _____		

FIGURE 5.11

A Sample Account Planning Tool

Of course, discretion is advised. We've time and again examined clients' account plans only to find pages of extraneous data. We always ask them, "What are those random pieces of information doing in there?" And the answer is always the same: "Because one person thought we needed it." As with any type of planning tool, there is merit in keeping things simple.

Common Issues. Companies that are heavily engaged in Account Management will tell you how important the process is to retaining and growing key accounts. And if the majority of your profits come from a small number of customers, it is nothing short of a necessity. But even in organizations that view Account Management as a mission-critical process, we still find two widespread behaviors that diminish the value of their sales forces' efforts.

The first misbehavior is treating Account Management like an annual event. Many, many companies invest lots of time in account planning toward the end of the calendar year, only to let their account plans sit on the shelf like an annual report. The work that went into them was solid, and the action plans would have a great impact on the targeted accounts, if the plans were ever executed.

Like Opportunity Management, Account Management is an iterative process. Though the heavy planning takes place at a defined interval (most commonly once a year), the activities are ongoing, and the account plan is a living document. If the plans are not used as operational guidelines for the account and updated frequently, they are little more than annual intermissions of strategic thinking separated by long expanses of random actions. If Account Management is important to your organization, then do it. If not, then do not. But don't find yourself in the middle ground of investing moderate effort with zero return.

The second Account Management misbehavior is failing to involve customers in the process. To some, this may seem like an outlandish proposition. Why ever would you involve a customer in your account planning activities? Because that's the *only* way to gain strategic alignment between the two organizations and maximize the mutual benefit of the relationship. Let us give you an example of when neglecting this fact wasted *a lot* of one company's resources.

We were recently examining the Account Management processes of a major corporation, and its executives were explaining to us the tensions between its sales force and one of its largest customers. The customer had been with the company for more than a decade and was generating more than $100 million in revenue each year. The company had an entire team of salespeople and customer service reps dedicated to this single customer—however, things were not good.

Company Sales Executive: *For a number of reasons, our relationship with this account has really soured over the last couple of years.*

Vantage Point Performance: *What have you done to try to mend the wounds?*

Executive: *Well, you know that this major account doesn't actually consume the product that we sell them—they bundle it with their own products and resell it to their customers as a packaged solution. The end customer knows us by name but doesn't purchase directly from us.*

VPP: *Yes. We understand. Your product is used by your major account's customers.*

Executive: *Right. So this year we launched a huge initiative to get to know our customer's customers—the ones who actually use our product. The reasoning was that if we could improve the end users' experience with our product, then it would also improve their experience with our major account's products. Our major account had complained about the end users' experience in the past, so it made a lot of sense.*

VPP: *And how is it going?*

Executive: *It's a disaster.*

VPP: *Why?*

Executive: *The major account said it didn't want us to do it.*

VPP: *What do you mean, it didn't want you do to it?*

Executive: *Their leadership team said that there were other operational issues they wanted us to focus on instead.*

VPP: *But, weren't they the ones who asked you to get to know their customers?*

Executive: *No. They didn't ask us. We just thought it was the right thing to do.*

VPP: *So, you launched that entire initiative without any input from your major account?*

Executive: *Yes, and it didn't help our relationship at all. They are really very upset about the operational issues.*

VPP: *Didn't that come out in your account planning discussions with them at the end of last year?*

Executive: *No. We don't typically involve customers in our planning processes.*

VPP: *Why not? Wouldn't involving them in the process have prevented you from wasting a lot of time and money this year?*

Executive: *Yeah. Probably. That's perhaps something we should consider doing in the future.*

VPP: *I'd say that's definitely something to consider.*

Failing to include its major customer in their Account Management activities not only caused our client to waste lots of resources on an unwanted initiative, it distracted executives from making operational improvements that would have helped to heal their fractured relationship. You can only align your sales force's efforts with your customers' objectives if you collaborate during account planning activities. If nothing else, it might be something to consider.

Territory Management

With rare exception, salespeople are responsible for selling to more than a single customer. In fact, sales reps will frequently have a database with hundreds of prospects and customers that they contact on a routine basis. Whether organized by geography, industry, size, or some other corporate characteristic, most salespeople are assigned a defined group of target customers. This group of targets is commonly referred to as a *sales territory*.

Anyone who has ever owned a sales territory can attest that there is never enough time to fully serve all of these prospects and customers. And even if there were, certain customers deserve more attention than others. Therefore, one of the most important decisions a seller has to make on a daily basis is this: *How do I allocate my time across all of the customers in my territory?* This process of identifying, prioritizing, and calling on target customers is called *Territory Management*.

The Activities. While the first three sales processes we explored are designed to increase the *effectiveness* of a salesperson's effort, Territory Management is all about *efficiency*. Stated in more tactical terms, Call, Opportunity, and Account Management processes help your salespeople *improve* what they do when they are face-to-face with a customer. Territory Management helps sellers *get face-to-face* with as many qualified customers as possible given their time and resource constraints. If you only have so many hours each day to call on customers, you'd better use them wisely.

The first activity in managing a territory is to *prioritize your customers*. Without a clear customer hierarchy, all customers look alike to a sales force. Customer prioritization should be determined by your company's current Customer Focus objectives. Whether the Sales Objective is to win customers in a particular industry, acquire customers that buy certain products, or grow revenue from existing customers, your Customer Focus should determine how you identify high-priority customers. And if your Customer Focus objectives happen to change over time, then so should your Territory Management priorities. You need to know your target before you can hit it.

The second Territory Management activity is to *define the territory*. Despite the fact the word *territory* in everyday language refers to a geographic patch of land, in the world of sales, a territory can be virtual. That is, a salesperson could be assigned a territory that is a handful of accounts spread all across the globe. Customers in a territory do not have to be in close proximity to one another; they simply have to be assigned to a rep.

Some companies choose to redefine their sales territories on a periodic basis—say annually. Others do so only as circumstances change—when they hire new salespeople, shift their Customer Focus, or perceive changes in the marketplace. Regardless of how frequently you reconfigure your territories, making sure that the territories are configured properly for each sales rep is a vital step toward good territory management.

The third activity is to *design customer call patterns*. These are the tactical plans that communicate the frequency with which certain types of customers are to be called. For instance, if your Customer Focus objective for the year is to acquire *new* customers, then you might choose to direct more of your sales calls toward prospects than toward existing customers. If your objective happens to change to increasing Share of Wallet with current customers, then your priorities would shift, and you would reallocate those sales calls back toward existing accounts. With this example, you can begin to see how managing Sales Activities so powerfully affects the attainment of specific Sales Objectives.

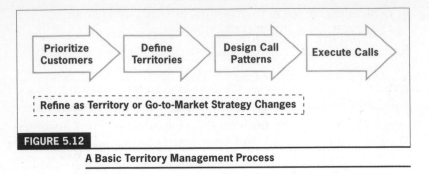

FIGURE 5.12

A Basic Territory Management Process

Finally, your sales force must *execute* its designated call patterns according to plan. When call patterns are closely followed, the sales force becomes that nimble strategic weapon that can be confidently redirected as circumstances change. But when call patterns break down, the sales force becomes an unguided brute, hitting its target only by luck or providence. An undisciplined sales force not only makes inefficient use of your sales force's effort, it can also threaten the achievement of your company's stated Sales Objectives.

It is worth reiterating that Territory Management is subject to constant refinement. As market dynamics or Sales Objectives change, you should reengineer your territories and redesign your call patterns (see Figure 5.12). Particularly if your company has constantly evolving product and customer priorities, we cannot overstate the importance of keeping Territory Management activities aligned with your Sales Objectives. Otherwise, your sales force may be dutifully executing *last year's* strategy.

Also, we should mention that the first three Territory Management activities are often performed by the organization *for* the salesperson. Defining territories, prioritizing customers, and even designing call patterns involve a level of analytics and organizational alignment that are perhaps best done by sales management or a sales operations support group. However, the accurate execution of the call pattern is unquestionably the responsibility of the salespeople, and they must be held accountable in order for your market-facing objectives to be met.

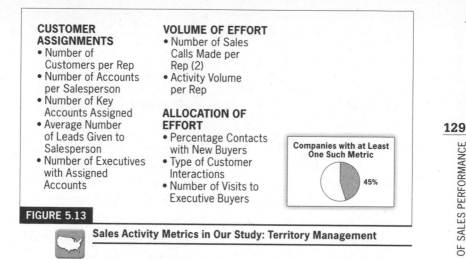

CUSTOMER ASSIGNMENTS
- Number of Customers per Rep
- Number of Accounts per Salesperson
- Number of Key Accounts Assigned
- Average Number of Leads Given to Salesperson
- Number of Executives with Assigned Accounts

VOLUME OF EFFORT
- Number of Sales Calls Made per Rep (2)
- Activity Volume per Rep

ALLOCATION OF EFFORT
- Percentage Contacts with New Buyers
- Type of Customer Interactions
- Number of Visits to Executive Buyers

Companies with at Least One Such Metric
45%

FIGURE 5.13

Sales Activity Metrics in Our Study: Territory Management

The Metrics. In our research, we noted three distinct types of Territory Management metrics (see Figure 5.13). The first measures activities toward the front of the process—*assigning customers and prospects to the sales force.* Metrics such as Number of Customers per Rep and Number of Key Accounts Assigned are intended to ensure that customers and prospects are assigned to sales reps in the correct quantity and ratio. Too many customers, too few customers, or unassigned customers can lead to an inefficient selling effort.

The second type of metric focuses on the *volume of effort* that salespeople are applying to their territories. Measures such as Number of Calls Made or Activity Volume per Rep represent the most "old-school" of old-school metrics. They reveal how hard your salespeople are running but not in which direction.

The third and final flavor of Territory Management metrics are the type that we find most useful because they reflect the sales force's *allocation of effort* across a company's desired targets. Numbers such as Percentage Contact with New Buyers and Type of Customer Interactions shed light on how salespeople are investing their time across different types of buyers and different types of sales calls. If acquiring new customers is one of your Sales Objectives, then you do not only want to know how many calls your sellers are making—you want to know how many calls they are making *on prospects*. Metrics like this transform the old school into higher education.

The Tools. Unlike Call, Opportunity, and Account Management activities that are performed continuously in the field, most Territory Management activities are completed on a periodic basis and often by a centralized group. Consequently, a company can afford to spend a lot of time trying to get its Territory Management strategies and tactics correct. And since these decisions lend themselves to in-depth quantitative analysis, very sophisticated analytic tools have been developed to support this process.

Territory definition is probably the most quantitative exercise in the Territory Management process. Ideally, each salesperson's territory would be perfectly sized to utilize 100% of his available time to call on customers, *and* his mix of customers and prospects would perfectly mirror your company's Customer Focus objectives. While some companies simply assign convenient chunks of geography to their salespeople with little regard for the territory's composition, other companies scrutinize travel time and salesperson availability down to the minute in an attempt to create perfect territories. We've worked with companies at both extremes and tend to prefer a more analytic approach, within the boundaries of reason.

The most common tool to use to prioritize customers and design call patterns is the electronic spreadsheet (see Figure 5.14). Since the goal of these activities is to determine which customers are most desirable and how many sales calls can be allocated to each, spreadsheets are useful for the many iterative calculations required to reach agreement on the actual targets and the distribution of salesperson effort. As always, which tool you use is not as important as the deliberate thought that goes into making these critical decisions.

Executing the call patterns is of course a very manual activity. You could say that the tools here are the salesperson's means of transportation and communication: planes, trains, and automobiles. Phones, computers, and mail. The tools of choice are any means that will get the seller most efficiently in front of her target customers and prospects.

TARGET CALL PATTERN						
		# Face-to-Face Visits per Year				
Coverage Level	Customer Segment	Sales Rep	Technical Rep	Sales Manager	Regional VP	Vice President
High Touch	National Accounts	12	6	4		2
	Very Large	12	6		2	1
Moderate Touch	Large	6	4	4	2	
	Medium	4	2	2	1	
Low Touch	Small	2	as needed			
Minimum	Very Small	1				

FIGURE 5.14

A Sample Call-Pattern Design Tool

Common Issues. When companies choose to engage in Territory Management, the issues are rarely with the analytics. Sales leadership is more than capable of designing adequate territories and call patterns. The problems arise in the execution of the call patterns, and there are two issues that are particularly meddlesome.

The most disruptive factor in call pattern execution is "firefighting." Despite the best-laid plans for proactive, high-value sales calls, salespeople with assigned accounts are susceptible to becoming full-time troubleshooters for their customers. Even in organizations with dedicated customer support roles, the salesperson is still the primary firefighter in the mind of the customer. And there is always a fire smoldering somewhere.

This problem can only be resolved through self-restraint by both salespeople and their managers. To be practical, some level of customer service is inherent in many selling roles. However, it should be meted out in the bare-minimum quantity *and* only to high-priority issues. If every customer can send its sales rep in search of a corrected invoice, then sales force call patterns don't need to be directed toward external customers—they need to be directed at finance, operations, and every other internal corporate function.[4]

---

4. We once had a client whose customers held firefighting in such high regard that they allotted a meaningful amount of time in their call patterns to "reactive" sales calls. Though it caused us some consternation, it did allow them to design realistic territories and set attainable targets for their reps.

The second issue that destroys the integrity of good Territory Management has been mentioned previously, the hit-your-number-any-way-you-can mentality demonstrated by a lot of management teams. In pursuit of the ultimate Business Results, objectives like Market Coverage and Customer Focus get disregarded by those who perceive a different path to success.

When the generals in the war room order their troops to capture a hill, it's unacceptable for the troops to capture a valley instead. Even if the leaders on the ground can claim that it's a bigger plot of land and they incurred fewer casualties, the troops deviated from a strategic plan that was carefully designed to win the overall war. They put the greater outcome at risk in order to achieve an easier near-term objective. That's why there is a war room in the first place—to make sure that the many individual battles are coordinated and building toward an eventual victory.

If you believe that the wise allocation of sales calls will substantially affect your sales force's productivity, then you should put the appropriate processes, tools, and metrics in place for effective Territory Management and then make it happen. Communicate your expectations, and inspect that they are being met. As with any sales process, discipline is required to reap big rewards.

Sales Force Enablement

We've made the case that management rigor is a key driver of sales force performance. With focused attention on how calls, opportunities, accounts, and territories are managed, sales leadership can steer its teams most directly toward its company's desired Sales Objectives and Business Results. In other words, sales success is built on sound execution of the right Sales Activities.

However, all of these activities are executed by individuals, and the capability of those individuals plays a tremendous role in the soundness of their execution. Although we still encounter unenlightened companies that treat their salespeople as

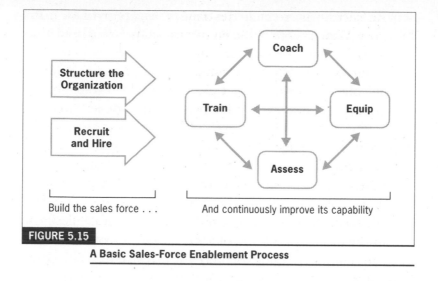

FIGURE 5.15

A Basic Sales-Force Enablement Process

disposable commodities, the vast majority of sales leaders today recognize that highly capable sellers are worth their weight in Business Results. Consequently, they invest heavily in their sales forces to build their capabilities and improve execution in the field. This process of investing in improved sales execution is called *Sales Force Enablement*.

The Activities. As we mentioned in Chapter 4, Sales Force Capability is more than just the skill of the sales force—it also encompasses the greater system in which salespeople operate. This includes the strategies the salespeople employ, the processes they follow, the tools that support their activities, the expectations that are communicated to them, and many other elements that go well beyond the scope of only training to develop skills. Capability basically incorporates every aspect of how a salesperson does her job. Accordingly, Sales Force Enablement includes a variety of tactics that an organization can use to increase its sales force's ability to execute (see Figure 5.15).

First, management should *structure the organization* in a way that provides its salespeople with access to the resources they need to perform their jobs efficiently and effectively. If the sales manager plays a pivotal role in your seller's day-to-day activities, then where you locate your managers and how many reps you assign to each will have a great impact on salesperson performance. Or if your typical sale involves roles such as technical engineers or other specialists, then easy access to those individuals is a must-have for your salespeople. The coordination of internal resources is often required in complex sales, and organization structure can influence it tremendously.

Second, you must *recruit and hire* salespeople to staff your organization appropriately. If your sales force is chock-full of talented sellers, then the burden on every other Sales Enablement activity is reduced. But if your sales force is ladened with mediocrity, you will have to invest heavily to elevate sales performance. We should note that recruiting and hiring not only has a direct impact on the objective of Sales Force Capability but also on Market Coverage. Having the right number of skilled salespeople onboard makes a manager's world a much happier place.

Clearly, you need to *train your sales force* to develop the skills and knowledge necessary to capably execute its Sales Activities. Training is the most widely used means of Sales Force Enablement, and it is a very efficient way to fill capability gaps that are common across a sales force. Training is so deeply embedded in the sales culture that it really requires little explanation.

Another way to develop your salespeople's skills and knowledge is to *coach them individually.* Whereas training is designed to instill common knowledge across a sales force, coaching is used to build a salesperson's abilities based on her unique development needs. As Sales Force Enablement activities go, this is the most value-added of them all. Unfortunately, it's also the most time-intensive for a manager, so it must be done in a deliberate and thoughtful way.

You also must *equip your salespeople* with tools or job aids that support their selling activities. From sales presentations, to proposal templates, to communication devices, and a vast assortment of other documents and gadgets, salespeople have more tools in their hands today than ever before. Organizations have discovered that equipping their sales forces with relevant tools is a high-leverage investment that promotes consistent execution across an organization.

The final Sales Force Enablement activity found in our research is to *assess the sales force*. Sales force assessment can be done in many different ways using many different tools and methodologies. We prefer to use a combination of assessments to get several perspectives on potential issues—both at the individual and organizational levels. However you go about it, assessing the capability of your sales force has broad implications for how you approach the other enablement activities.

As you might have concluded, the Sales Force Enablement "process" is really a collection of ongoing activities. Some activities such as coaching should be done on a never-ending basis, though few companies coach enough. Others, such as restructuring the sales organization, can be done episodically, though we know companies that scramble their org charts almost daily. These activities are also highly interrelated; for instance, you could train someone on how to use a new sales tool and then reinforce that skill with coaching. The greater point is that there is a selection of Sales Activities in which sales management can make deliberate investments to achieve specific Sales Objectives.

To give an example, if you set an objective for the year to increase your Percentage of Proposals Won, there are several Sales Enablement activities that you could use as levers:

- Recruit and hire dedicated proposal writers to review and edit all proposals.
- Structure your team so that each region has its own proposal writer.
- Equip your sales force with proposal templates for different types of products or customers.
- Train your salespeople on how to use the templates.
- Coach them through the development of several proposals.
- Assess their proposal writing skills at regular intervals.
- Refine all of the above based on your results.

If you took an approach like this, it would seem impossible for you *not* to make progress toward your objective. And there are probably dozens of other activities that you could also undertake requiring varying levels of investment. But you can see how a robust Sales Force Enablement effort that is focused on a specific Sales Objective will have a predictable and profound impact on your sales force's performance.

It's worth mentioning that Sales Force Enablement activities are not the sole domain of the sales force. While they are typically overseen by sales management, they can also be owned or supported by human resources, information technology, or other corporate functions with the appropriate competencies. In fact, many of these activities can be outsourced, as we do a fair amount of assessing, training, and coaching sales forces for our clients. Regardless of who carries out the activities, sales management should be responsible for setting the Sales Force Enablement agenda and then measuring its outcomes.

The Metrics. Of all the Sales Activities numbers on our wall, Sales Force Enablement metrics were the most prevalent by far—representing more than 50% of the activity-level measures. Since the metrics themselves revealed the activities we just described, we of course observed metrics that aligned with each activity (see Figure 5.16).

With regard to organization structure, we found metrics such as Manager Span of Control and Ratio of Salespeople to Sales Support. These measures show whether staffing levels are in balance among various resources for the salesperson. By providing sellers with adequate oversight and support, leadership helps its reps function at full capacity.

We witnessed only one hiring metric study, which was Recruiting Spend per FTE. However, we have known companies that track things like Number of Recruiting Events Held, Number of Candidates Interviewed, and other measures of recruiting activity to make sure their pipeline of potential employees remains full.

Roughly half of the Sales Force Enablement numbers on the wall were intended to measure some aspect of sales training. Metrics like Training Hours per FTE show the volume of training taking place, while numbers like Days of Training by

ORGANIZATION
- Number of Reps Assigned per Manager
- Ratio of Salespeople to Customer-Facing Sales Support

RECRUITING
- Recruiting Spend per FTE

TRAINING
- Training Hours per FTE (3)
- Training Investment per FTE
- Number of Trainings Completed
- Number of Training Hours
- Volume of Salesperson Training

- Days of Training by Type
- Percentage of Training Dollars by Type
- Hours of Training Delivered by Type
- Percentage with Training Completed
- Percentage of Salespeople with Certification
- Percentage of Certified Salespeople

COACHING
- Percentage of Time Spent Coaching
- Volume of Coaching
- Coaching Time
- Frequency of Coaching

TOOLS
- IT Spend per FTE
- Percentage Using Tools
- Percentage Using Reporting Capabilities
- Percentage of Users Logging into CRM
- Usage of SFA

ASSESSMENT
- Percentage of Salespeople Assessed
- Percentage of Performance Appraisals Complete

Companies with at Least One Such Metric

40%

FIGURE 5.16

Sales Activity Metrics in Our Study: Sales Force Enablement

Type put a finer lens on the precise types of skills that are being emphasized. A final type of training metric like Percentage of Certified Salespeople demonstrates that the sellers had completed a formal training program. It is clear from our research that leadership is very focused on monitoring its training investment.

We were pleased to find several coaching metrics in the mix, such as Percentage of Time Spent Coaching and Frequency of Coaching. As we mentioned previously, companies are increasingly expecting their sales managers to engage in active coaching. Measures such as these not only indicate that coaching is taking place, but they also force an organization to deliberately define what, why, when, where, and how it wants coaching to take place.

We were also encouraged to discover metrics on sales tools. Numbers such as IT Spend per FTE measure the level of investment a company is making in its supporting infrastructure, and metrics such as Percentage of Users Logging into SFA reveal whether or not the investment is being leveraged by the sales force. As we provide greater insight into the effective use of metrics, we hope that numbers like these gain in prominence.

The final type of Sales Force Enablement metric we encountered was pointed toward assessing the sales force. Measures like Percentage of Salespeople Assessed and Percentage of Performance Appraisals Complete can give management confidence that the sales force is at least aware of its own capability. Performance assessments are also essential to any ongoing continuous improvement efforts.

The Issues. The Sales Enablement activities that a company could potentially undertake are so diverse that we could write a separate book on the issues associated with this process. But let us highlight one that is particularly widespread and leads many companies to waste massive amounts of time and money. It is the ready-fire-aim approach that companies frequently take when deploying new Sales Enablement initiatives.

Any meaningful Sales Force Enablement program requires a large investment of company resources, and implementing real change can be very disruptive to a sales force. You would expect, then, that companies would be extremely careful to identify, analyze, and prioritize their sales improvement alternatives *before* making such consequential commitments on behalf of their sales forces. However, we know few companies that do a thorough job of assessing their sales forces' needs *before* charging into expensive change efforts that yield questionable returns on their investment. Such decisions are routinely made based on anecdote, inertia, or convenience, with predictably lackluster outcomes.

For instance, a company once asked us to help it redesign its sales processes as part of a larger sales-force automation project. Leadership was adamant that it needed an expensive new CRM tool, despite the fact that its sales force *loved* the company's existing system, and it had no major functional deficiencies. When we quizzed the leadership team on why it wanted the new CRM application, the leaders responded, "Well, this one is getting pretty old, and it's no longer best-practice." Whether or not that was true, we saw several other problems with its sales force that could have been fixed for a much smaller investment and with a much greater return. But the team had not assessed its Sales Force Enablement alternatives—it simply decided to replace the CRM tool. We don't know how these leaders got the itch, but they scratched it without looking at other more serious wounds.

A second example is one that we encounter repeatedly: the launching of a major sales training program without any analysis of the sales force's true enablement needs. We've talked more than one company *out* of conducting training that they approached us to facilitate because it was obvious to us that it wouldn't produce the results they were expecting. In some cases, we felt they had selected the wrong type of training, but in others, we determined that their issue wasn't even a deficiency of skill. They really needed better processes, tools, or other systemic contributors to sales performance. Training is often the easiest place to go for a Sales Enablement initiative, but it is not always the right destination. Though training your sales force on irrelevant skills probably won't harm your salespeople, it sure will waste their time. And your money.

The examples could go on, but the lesson would be the same: don't prescribe a remedy without first examining the patient—particularly when the remedy is an invasive procedure. There is no shortage of ways to enable a sales force, and no enablement activity is appropriate for every situation. Will sales training elevate the performance of your sales force? Sure, if it's the right training. Will providing new sales tools enable better selling? Sure, if they're the right tools. Will a ready-fire-aim approach to Sales Force Enablement deliver the results you desire? Sure, if you're lucky.

FACT: BETTER PROCESSES = BETTER SALES PERFORMANCE

A funny thing happens when we start talking to people about formalizing their sales processes. All of their energy and enthusiasm immediately disappears. It's as if the term *process* possesses the curious ability to suck all of the joy out of a room full of otherwise happy salespeople. In fact, should you ever want to destroy the cheerful atmosphere at your annual holiday party, just stand in front of the room and list all of the new sales processes you'll be implementing in the coming year. Joy vacuum, activated.

Fortunately, our friends at the sales performance benchmarking firm CSO Insights have some information that might help reinflate the room's spirits. Their research reveals that those very processes could help you sell 23% more stuff next year. That's right, sales process really is a good thing.

Each year CSO Insights surveys thousands of sales forces around the world and collects data on their sales force's demographics, management practices, and sales reps' performance. It then compiles that data to allow its customers to benchmark their own performance against peer organizations in areas such as quota attainment, compensation strategies, CRM usage, sales methodology, and a variety of other meaningful topics.

Among its areas of inquiry, CSO Insights asks its respondents to rate their company's degree of sales process implementation among four levels of sophistication:

1. **Ad hoc process:** The company lacks a single standard process, and each rep sells as he thinks best.
2. **Informal process:** The company gives its salespeople a sales process and expects them to follow it, but usage is neither monitored nor measured.
3. **Formal process:** The company enforces the use of a defined sales process and periodically reviews the process to ensure its effectiveness.
4. **Dynamic process:** The company monitors and provides continuous feedback on sales reps' usage of the process and proactively modifies the process when market conditions change.

As you might expect, a minority of companies have deployed rigorous sales processes, with almost 60% of the respondents claiming that their processes are either ad hoc or informal (see Figure 5.17). We believe these low levels of rigor are insufficient

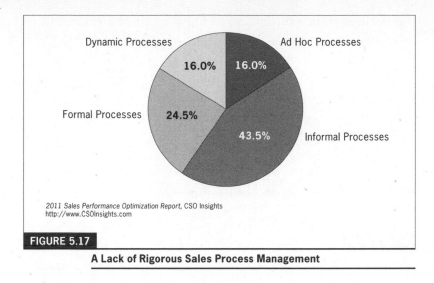

2011 Sales Performance Optimization Report, CSO Insights
http://www.CSOInsights.com

FIGURE 5.17

A Lack of Rigorous Sales Process Management

to exert substantial influence over sales performance, which means that 60% of these sales managers are missing fundamental management tools. Even more distressing, this number has decreased by only 2.5% over the past five years. The sales process revolution has apparently been accelerating at a pretty slow pace.

A more encouraging story was told when CSO Insights examined the payoff for the enlightened 40% that had implemented formal or dynamic sales processes. When these levels of sales process implementation were correlated with each company's actual performance, CSO Insights discovered the following:

> **Companies with more developed sales processes enjoy greater sales performance.**

In fact, sales forces in the 2011 study with "dynamic" processes won 53% of their forecasted deals compared to 43% in their peers with "ad hoc" processes (see Figure 5.18). All other things being equal, that means that rigorous sales process management yielded 23% more output from a sales force.[5] Now that's a reason to celebrate.

---

5. 53% ÷ 43% = 123%

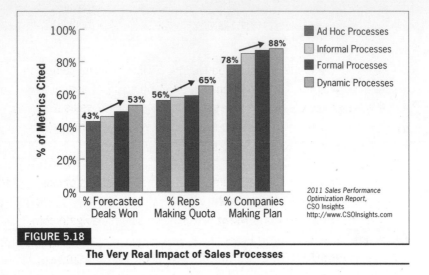

2011 Sales Performance
Optimization Report,
CSO Insights
http://www.CSOInsights.com

FIGURE 5.18

The Very Real Impact of Sales Processes

Similarly, 65% of sales reps in companies with more rigorous processes achieved their quota, compared to 56% in the more lackadaisical sales forces. And 88% of the dynamic-process companies reached their company's overall sales goal, compared to 78% in the ad hoc group. Viewed from nearly every possible angle, CSO Insight's research consistently confirms that better sales processes equal better sales performance.

So while a new sales process may not be at the top of every sales force's wish list, there's no disputing the fact that performance improves when the right sales processes are properly implemented. And improved sales performance probably *is* on those wish lists. So let us now explore how you should go about identifying the right processes to amplify your own Business Results.

And then there were none.

All 306 of the metrics in our study had now found a home somewhere on our war room wall. The final pieces of the sales management code had been revealed in the Sales Activities layer of our sales management framework, with all of the activities falling neatly into one of five sales processes:

1. **Call Management**, which improves the effectiveness of individual customer interactions
2. **Opportunity Management**, which helps sellers navigate complex, multi-call sales cycles
3. **Account Management**, which maximizes the long-term value of a single customer
4. **Territory Management**, which allocates selling effort efficiently across numerous types of customers
5. **Sales Force Enablement**, which improves a sales force's ability to execute

These five processes and their related activities are the fundamental building blocks of control over sales performance because these are the things that you can actually manage. Unlike Sales Objectives and Business Results, Sales Activities can be directed by a sales manager. These numbers can be changed at will, and cleverly doing so will drive predictable improvement in overall sales performance (see Figure 5.19). As we've commented, this is where the action is.

Unfortunately, our research showed that these highly manageable metrics are in relatively low demand, with fewer than 20% of the numbers on our wall pointed at Sales Activities. Whether these numbers are difficult to obtain or whether leadership is just hesitant to collect them, they are missing from most companies' management toolbox. However, these numbers are the leading indicators of sales success, and they should be on everyone's war room wall. With them, you can begin to proactively manage your sales force. Without them, control will continue to elude you.

With the chaos on our wall now completely in order, we felt that we had finally cracked the sales management code. In our own sort of sales

SALES PROCESS	PURPOSE OF METRICS	SAMPLE METRICS
Call Management	Improve the quality of individual customer interactions	• % of Reps Doing Call Planning • Call Plan Usage • Average Talk Time
Opportunity Management	Initiate, qualify, advance, and close multistage sales	• # of Opportunity Plans Completed • Adherence to Opportunity Planning Process • % of Qualified Opportunities
Account Management	Maximize the long-term value of select customers	• # of Business Plans Completed • % of Account Plans in Place • # of Interactions per Account
Territory Management	Allocate selling effort efficiently across various types of customers and prospects	• # of Customers per Rep • # of Sales Calls Made per Rep • % of Contacts with New Buyers
Sales Force Enablement	Improve the sales force's ability to execute	• % of Time Spent Coaching • Training Hrs per FTE • % of Users Logging into CRM

FIGURE 5.19

Sales Activities with Corresponding Metrics

genome project, we had effectively mapped the sales force's DNA by forcing hundreds of seemingly random data points into a tidy framework of cause and effect (see Figure 5.20). We now knew which elements managers can control in a sales force and which they can't. We could see the inner workings of sales performance—the levers and pulleys that are used to drive a sales force down the path of management's choosing.

However, it wasn't yet a full set of operating instructions. To make the code practically useful, we would need to understand how the framework should be applied to the task of managing any particular sales force. We had the "superset" of things leadership could measure and manage, but we needed clear guidelines to help cull from it the handful of activities and metrics that would enable leadership to focus on its own organizational goals. We needed to know *how* to apply these insights in a targeted and tactical way. Fortunately, we were on the verge of doing just that.

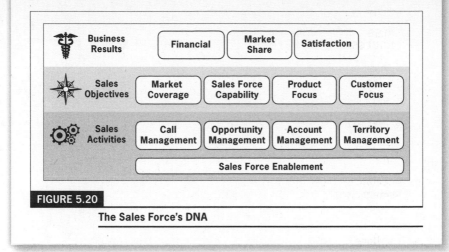

FIGURE 5.20

The Sales Force's DNA

PART 3

Using the Code to Manage *Your* Sales Force

Building the Foundation for Control

CHAPTER 6

THE BUILDING BLOCKS

We've made the point that sales processes are the building blocks of control over sales force performance. Since you can only truly manage your salespeople's activities, you must achieve your Sales Objectives and Business Results by implementing formal processes that you can tactically direct and measure. *With* process rigor, you can manage the territories, accounts, opportunities, and calls that lead to successful sales outcomes. Without process rigor, you are asking for the outcomes but leaving the critical tactics to chance.

This latter state of affairs is what faced senior executives at the $400 million software company we discussed in the previous chapter. The company's VP of sales had put rich incentives in place for his salespeople and then let them run free to sell as they wished. This "management by results" approach worked just fine when the market was growing wildly, but it crippled management's ability to control its sales force when the joy ride came to an end. When the managers ultimately needed the levers and pulleys to control sales performance, they found that their hands were empty.

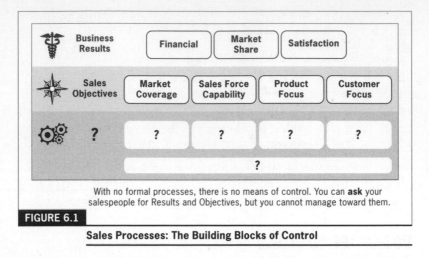

With no formal processes, there is no means of control. You can **ask** your salespeople for Results and Objectives, but you cannot manage toward them.

FIGURE 6.1

Sales Processes: The Building Blocks of Control

The software company's leadership soon came to the conclusion that "management by results" was not the best strategy. "Management of activities" is a much more satisfying way for executives to live their lives. Therefore, they went down the path of implementing formal sales processes to gain control of their sales performance. Starting with a blank page, they designed new sales processes that defined the way they wanted their salespeople to sell. Despite the fact that the company had already grown into a sizeable corporate entity, leadership returned to the most basic of decisions—what do we want our salespeople to do?

This is the kind of back-to-basics exercise that must be conducted before you can progress to the more advanced task of architecting a system of metrics that will allow you to attain your desired Business Results. To fully avail yourself of the newly cracked sales management code, you must first put in place the formal processes that will enable you to proficiently measure and manage your Sales Activities. Even if you already have a formal process in place, we encourage you to review your current state of affairs to make certain you're working from a solid foundation. Until the levers and pulleys are in place for you to control the selling effort, you will necessarily remain in a management-by-results quandary (see Figure 6.1).

With increasing frequency, executives are coming to us for these exact reasons—either to implement formal sales processes for the first time or to reexamine their existing processes and make them more potent. This tells us that sales has finally turned the corner toward a structured management discipline and leaders are now reaching for the levers and pulleys to take control of their sales forces. And as we work with them to explore their companies' process needs, they invariably ask a question that has been posed to us many times: "Which sales process is best for our company?"

WHICH SALES PROCESS IS BEST FOR OUR COMPANY?

It seems to be a reasonable question. If we know all of the facts about our company, how hard can it be to choose a process that will best fit our sales force? Unfortunately, it's not only hard to answer this common question, it is impossible. And the reason the question is impossible to answer is because it's *the wrong question to ask*. Let us share another client experience that will illustrate why this is the case.

One of our own repeat customers once asked us to help redesign the company's training curriculum for frontline sales managers. Leadership had decided that the company's existing training modules were too generic (which they were), and it wanted to build something more focused on the way its sales force actually sells. More specifically, it wanted to move away from teaching generalized coaching skills and focus all of its manager training on the actual activities of its salespeople. The company's executives felt this would prepare their managers to provide more relevant coaching in the field and to reinforce specific behaviors that were known to be important. From our perspective, they had formed a brilliant plan. So far, so good.

But they went on to say that they thought the challenge of coaching salespeople would be easier if all of their sellers used a common sales methodology. This would promote uniformity across their company—both in their overall sales approach and the management of their salespeople. Therefore, they wanted us to help them develop a single sales process that they could deploy across their entire organization. A single sales process, for their entire organization. Unknowingly, they had just ruined their previously stellar plan. So far, not so good.

They'd effectively asked us the question, Which sales process is best for our company? To understand why this was a bad question to ask, consider that this is a multibillion-dollar global conglomerate with dozens of sales forces selling dozens of different products to thousands of different customers. Even within a single sales force, they might have several different types of salespeople, each doing different things. For example, one of their sales forces includes geographic sales reps who manage territories, lead generators who manage cold calls, as well as strategic account managers who manage major customers. How could they ever design a single sales process that would be relevant for every salesperson in this sales force—let alone the entire company? They couldn't. It would be impossible. No single sales process could help them manage all of their various selling roles, because each role has its own unique activities that are driving toward unique goals. This is why it's almost always futile to ask which sales process is best for a *company*.

Unless the company has only one sales role and all of its sellers do exactly the same things, no common sales process will do the job. The *right* question to ask when you are selecting a sales process is, Which process is right for this specific role in my sales force? Not what is right for your entire company—just for a single role. This is an extremely critical point to understand as you begin to implement or redesign your formal sales processes:

> **The specific sales processes you need in your sales force are determined by the *nature of each individual selling role*.**

This might appear to be a game of semantics, differentiating between a company's sales force and its individual selling roles, but it is anything but that. What good would a company-wide

Account Management process do for a salesperson making 50 outbound lead-generation phone calls each day? None. And what good would a company-wide Territory Management process do for a strategic account manager who has only one assigned account? None. Yet how many times do you think companies deploy Account Management processes across every role in their sales force? Many. And how often does sales management try to track the time allocation of its major account managers? Often. These are all well-intentioned management errors but errors nonetheless.

This can be another brick-meet-forehead moment for sales leaders—that different selling roles require different sales processes. Which formal processes you deploy should be determined by the nature of each distinct role in your sales force. If you choose the *right* processes, what you are attempting to measure and manage will align naturally with the activities of your sellers. If you choose the wrong sales processes, the numbers on your war room walls will produce nothing but noise. And that noise will be screams from the battlefield where your sales force is being asked to do unnatural things.

From the perspective of salespeople in the field, being measured and managed in ways that don't align with their known world is exceedingly frustrating. It not only causes them to resent being made to follow misaligned processes, it raises suspicions that leadership isn't in tune with the reality on the ground. We once interviewed a sales manager who demonstrated symptoms of such a frustrating situation.

> **Vantage Point Performance:** *So, tell me a little bit about what your salespeople do. What are their primary activities?*
>
> **Frustrated Sales Manager:** *Well, they're basically account managers. Each of them is assigned to one of our major customers, and they're responsible for structuring the business relationship between our two companies and then ensuring that things operate smoothly throughout the year. They troubleshoot a lot and generally make sure that their accounts are happy.*
>
> **VPP:** *Sounds pretty straightforward. And how do you know if they're doing a good job? How do you measure their success?*

Manager: *We have a performance report that's generated from our CRM tool. At the beginning of each month, it's sent to both the senior leadership team and me.*

VPP: *And what are the key metrics on the report that you find most useful?*

Manager: *Me? None of them. The numbers on the report aren't that relevant for me or my salespeople. They're really just for the leadership team to see.*

VPP: *I'm not sure I understand.*

Manager: *The numbers on the report are things like Volume of Sales Calls Made, Length of Sales Cycle, and a bunch of other stuff that doesn't really apply to my group. They might be relevant for some of the other sales groups that have territory managers or whatever, but they don't help me manage my people any better.*

VPP: *Then why do you report a bunch of numbers that aren't relevant to your salespeople?*

Manager: *Our leadership team wants to have a single set of metrics that they can use to track our company's performance. I suspect that for most of our sales forces, these metrics work just fine. But my folks don't need to make hundreds of sales calls, and they don't really have sales cycles in the traditional sense. So I collect my own set of metrics that I keep in a separate spreadsheet.*

VPP: *You have your own sales metrics that you use to manage your sales force?*

Manager: *Yes.*

VPP: *Wouldn't your leadership team be interested to see the metrics that are actually important to your team's success?*

Manager: *No. I've asked them about it several times, but they seem intent on managing the entire sales force the same way. Honestly, I don't think they really understand what goes on in my group, since it's so unlike the other parts of the organization—which is a little ironic, since a high percentage of our overall revenue comes through my team. I guess as long as the top-line number looks good, they don't really care about the other metrics. Regardless, I have the metrics I need to manage my salespeople, and they have a handful of meaningless reports.*

This sales manager inherently understood that different selling roles follow different sales processes, and consequently they require different performance metrics to manage them effectively. Meanwhile, the leadership team unintentionally demonstrated that attempting to measure and manage salespeople with a set of irrelevant metrics creates noise on the war room wall and discontent in the field. In this case, the company was lucky to have an enlightened manager who took it upon himself to measure and manage his team appropriately. Unfortunately, not all companies are this lucky.

As this example illustrates, companies don't need sales processes; individual selling roles do. Attempting to manage an entire sales force in a uniform fashion neglects the unique activities of each sales role and diminishes management's effectiveness. His team needed an Account Management process—not the Territory Management process that was being used by his peer groups. So he abandoned the "company" sales process and effectively implemented his own. OK, not necessarily a tragedy. But it *is* a tragedy that his leadership team was in a war room somewhere staring at useless data on their wall. They had no visibility into the actual inner workings of his sales force, and they certainly had no control over his team's sales performance. Lots of data, no control.

So when someone asks, "Which sales process is best for our company?" he is asking the wrong question. The first question to ask when you begin to build or rebuild the foundation of your sales force is:

> **Which distinct selling roles
> are at work in our sales force?**

Answering this question will allow you to identify the nature of each selling role and to pinpoint the activities that drive success in each. With the roles and activities clearly defined, you can then turn to the more tactical question:

> **What is the best sales process to measure
> and manage each of my selling roles?**

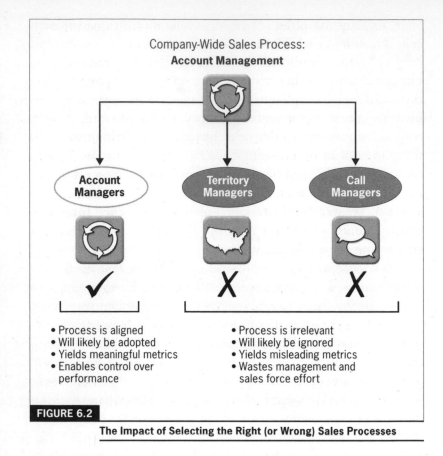

FIGURE 6.2

The Impact of Selecting the Right (or Wrong) Sales Processes

Answering this question will allow you to select the right sales processes to take control of your sales force's performance. Failing to answer this question will lead to two predictable situations—neither of which you will want to endure (see Figure 6.2).

The first thing that predictably happens when a mismatched process is forced onto a selling role is exactly what happened in the previous example—it will be ignored. So often when we hear executives grumble about low process adoption by their sellers, we discover that an irrelevant process has been dropped on top of a helpless sales role. Even if a territory manager *wanted* to use an Account Management process, he'd struggle to make it work. The struggle is usually fairly short, though, and the territory manager will minimize the process to the point of abandonment. It's often not the salesperson's fault that the process isn't being used. It's just the wrong process.

The second predictable consequence of an errant process implementation is that management will begin to exert effort trying to force compliance by the sellers. We've seen management spend an insane amount of time trying to train, deploy, retrain, and redeploy sales processes and supporting tools that will never be adopted—not because the training or deployment was botched, but because it botched the process selection. Implementing a formal sales process is not a trivial endeavor, and the greater the initial investment, the more intensely management wants it to pay off. It fights the battle with great energy, but the battle was lost before it began.

We once witnessed a tragic instance when *both* of these consequences were suffered by a well-intentioned management team. The company began its tragedy by implementing a Call Management process that it was convinced was needed by its territory sales reps. Unfortunately, the reps found no value in the process and immediately disregarded it. Realizing that the process implementation was a failure, the management team regrouped to assess what had gone wrong. Rather than reaching the proper conclusion that they had deployed an inappropriate process, they determined that the manual call planning activities were too burdensome on the reps, so they needed to automate the process within their CRM tool. Thus began an IT development project that would cost several hundred thousand dollars. Six months later, still no usage by the sales reps. Big investment, no adoption. Even bigger investment, still no adoption. All brought about by a fundamentally mismatched sales process.

In short, don't make the classic mistake of foisting formal processes on your sales force without vetting the individual selling roles and their critical Sales Activities. If you get a sales process implementation wrong, you could suffer through the mistake for years to come. But if you get it right, you'll enjoy a degree of control that will not only be evident in the war room, it will also be evident in the field. You will have a perfectly aligned sales management model.

Identifying Your Sales Roles

Your first step on the path to control is therefore to clearly delineate the various selling roles that reside within your organization. This is usually a relatively simple task, since distinct roles frequently have different titles and reporting relationships from one another. However, this is not always the case—particularly in companies that have merged or acquired other companies in the past. There can be a jumble of dotted lines and ambiguous titles that disguise the true nature of the selling roles. In those cases, you must look beyond the job title and org chart to assess what the sellers actually do.

There are an infinite number of ways to define selling roles, and we will not try to characterize every possible distinction. Here, common sense should prevail. But here are some typical reasons that sales roles are separated:

Different Customer Focus
- New vs. existing customers
- Large vs. small accounts
- High-priority vs. low-priority targets
- Executive vs. low-level buyers

Different Product Focus
- High- vs. low-tech products
- Stand-alone vs. bundled products

Different Buying/Selling Processes
- Consultative vs. transactional sales
- Long vs. short sales cycles
- Government vs. corporate buyers

Different Role in the Sales Cycle
- Lead generation vs. opportunity follow-up
- Opportunity managers vs. subject matter experts

Whatever the drivers of role distinction in your organization, you must ask yourself, What do these people actually do? What are their objectives, and what are their critical day-to-day selling activities? For example, two people with different titles who are both charged with canvassing a moderate number of existing customers may actually fit into a single "role" for the purposes of sales process selection. One client of ours had acquired numerous companies over the course of a decade, and it claimed to have more than 100 different roles in its sales force. We'll admit that there were probably 100 different titles on their business cards, but the actual number of distinct *roles* in play was fewer by an order of magnitude.

Alternatively, two people with the same title may really represent different roles. If one "account manager" makes hundreds of outbound phone calls per month, while another conducts only a handful of face-to-face meetings, we'd have to conclude that these are distinct roles engaged in quite different day-to-day activities. Therefore, we would distinguish between the two when determining which sales processes would be most appropriate to measure and manage their performance.

Regardless of nominal titles and organizational relationships, you need to assess which distinct selling roles reside in your organization before you can proceed to process matchmaking. Companies don't need sales processes—individual selling roles do. If you try to layer the same process on top of sellers with different tasks before them, at least one of the groups will end up resenting the process and potentially you, as well. Either way, you'll have made no forward progress toward a more manageable sales force.

Who Needs a Process?

Once you have identified the nature of the roles in your sales force, the next step is to select the specific sales processes that are most appropriate for each. In the previous chapter, we shared how categorizing the Sales Activity numbers on our war room wall had revealed five discrete sales processes. By examining the metrics and what they were intended to measure, we were also able to deduce the key activities and goals of each process. As we considered these activities and goals in even greater depth, we were able to identify the context in which these processes are the most useful. We will now explore these situations, because if you understand the contextual value of each sales process, it will become apparent to you which of the processes your selling roles require.

Call Management. Remember that a Call Management process is intended to improve the quality of individual customer interactions through the thoughtful planning of a sales call. This helps a salesperson preview the upcoming interaction, identify desired outcomes, anticipate the conversation, and generally plan for any contingencies that might be reasonably predicted. While Call Management demands a higher investment in call preparation, the extra effort pays off when the seller is able to safely maneuver the inevitable zigs and zags of live contact with a customer.

At its heart, call planning is about gaining control of a potentially messy situation. It's about anticipating the expected *and* the unexpected things that could occur during the call and then preparing yourself to handle them both tactically and emotionally. It is about charting the course that you *want* to take during the call and then trying to remove as much uncertainty and risk as possible. It enables you to proceed confidently but with a healthy dose of caution.

So to understand when Call Management would be an appropriate sales process, we asked ourselves, What type of sales call would warrant such caution on the part of the seller? The obvious answer is a call for which a negative outcome will have a meaningful and unwanted consequence on the sale. There must be some gravity to the sales call, or else a salesperson could leave the outcome to chance and save herself the extra effort of planning. So foremost, Call Management is a relevant sales process if:

> **A single sales call can greatly affect the outcome of the sale.**

But wait a minute. Aren't all sales calls important? If a call isn't important, then why make it? The truth is, many selling roles are not filled with potentially lethal customer interactions. It's not that their roles aren't high-pressure, but many sellers' day-to-day activities have a high service component or a "stay in front of the customer" mission. Salespeople such as these often have large territories of customers where ongoing relationships take precedence over individual interactions. In sales roles such as these, not every call is a do-or-die situation. These salespeople certainly add value to the customer relationships, but the majority of their activities are *relatively* low-risk.

In other cases, one bad sales call can kill the deal. This is particularly true for prospecting calls, when a poor outcome typically means that the entire opportunity is dead on arrival. Another example of a high-risk sales call would be one in which you are delivering your final proposal to a major prospect, a situation probably worthy of a little preparation. There are many types of calls that warrant extra precaution, and these are situations in which call planning is an especially good idea.

Another type of interaction that is a candidate for Call Management is a call with a high degree of uncertainty as to how the conversation will unfold. If all of a seller's calls are very routine with a well-worn agenda, then no preparation is needed. Nearly every call will happen precisely as expected. However, when a call could potentially take many different turns, call planning helps the sales rep anticipate the unexpected—primarily the unpredictable behavior of a customer. Therefore, Call Management is also relevant if:

> **The content of sales calls is highly variable, and the customer's behavior is uncertain.**

But isn't every sales call different? If every call were alike, wouldn't you need an actor rather than a salesperson? Of course every sales call is unique, but to differing degrees. Nearly every salesperson has some calls that they would consider "routine"— the types of calls that they have made many times and are basically the same discussion again and again. A sales rep who makes 100 prospecting calls per week is probably using a similar approach in most of his calls. Not every call will follow the same path, but most of them will. And a territory sales rep who does product demonstrations may give the exact same presentation to every customer. Will the audience respond differently from one instance to the next? Maybe. Will these salespeople need to spend an hour planning for each rote presentation? Maybe not.

But then there are calls that can go in many possible directions. If the prospect or customer is relatively unknown to the seller, the salesperson might need to invest a lot of time beforehand researching the customer and anticipating its needs. Or if a strategic account manager meets with her customer's executive team only a few times a year, then the conversation is likely to be rich and cover many different topics. This is another situation in which thorough preparation can help the salesperson anticipate the zigs and zags of an uncontrolled interaction. The more varied the content of the call and the less certain the customer's behavior, the more appropriate Call Management becomes.

One final factor that affects the relevance of Call Management activities is highlighted by the example just given of a seller who makes 100 outbound calls per week. In this case, there is the practical matter that a salesperson making such a high volume of calls cannot realistically plan for all of them, or even many of them. Call planning is a time-consuming activity that can only be employed when the potential payoff exceeds the known cost. Therefore Call Management is also most appropriate if:

[**The sales role makes a low to moderate number of sales calls.**]

But what is a "moderate" number of calls? Five in a week? Twenty? Fifty? Clearly there is no right answer—to an extent, it's all relative. But if a salesperson is asked to create call plans for too many calls, it won't be long before the exercise becomes administrative and loses its value. Don't let that happen.

Of course, there is an inverse relationship between the volume of planning a salesperson can do and the level of effort that is put into each planning session. We would argue that a salesperson should *never* pick up a phone or walk through a door without at least posing a few critical questions to himself, such as, What is my objective? How am I going to open the conversation? and What is the buyer's motivation to speak with me? But as far as formal call planning sessions go, we've seen Call Management have the greatest impact with salespeople who deliberately plan for a few calls each week. If they try to do many more, they become full-time planners rather than full-time sellers. So judgment must be used on the part of sales leadership as to how realistic extensive Call Management is for a particular selling role.

Opportunity Management. An Opportunity Management process is intended to help sellers strategically pursue and win deals that involve complex buying behavior. They force a salesperson to take inventory of all the factors that could influence the deal, like the buying process, its participants, the competitors, and other contextual details. Once the landscape is known, the seller then devises an approach to win the opportunity and executes her plan of attack.

The situation in which a selling role would need to engage in Opportunity Management activities is probably the most apparent of all five sales processes. Opportunities are deals that entail multiple customer interactions before they can be won, as opposed to sales that can be made with a single sales call. Opportunities also frequently involve multiple stakeholders in the buyer's organization that have different roles in the process and differing agendas. All of this puts pressure on the salesperson to be deliberate in his treatment of the pursuit. Therefore, an Opportunity Management process is relevant if:

> **The sales role pursues complex, multistage deals.**

Again, it's fairly evident when this is the case. Does the typical sale for the salesperson require multiple sales calls over time? Then the role is a pretty good candidate for Opportunity

Management activities. It's really that simple. But we have a few observations that we should share before we move on.

By definition, an opportunity is an individual pursuit that has a discrete beginning, middle, and end. It pops onto the salesperson's radar screen as a lead and then proceeds through milestones on a linear path toward an inevitable "win" or "loss." This is not to be confused with Account Management, for which a salesperson may make many, many calls on a single account in an attempt to sustain an ongoing stream of business. We have known companies to confuse Opportunity and Account Management activities because they can look very similar—a salesperson making multiple calls on various stakeholders in a buying organization. But Opportunity Management is only relevant if the activities surround distinct deals, not ongoing relationships.

That being said, the pursuit of a new "account" can actually be a situation that employs Opportunity Management. For instance, we work with many sales forces whose primary objective is to recruit new customers into long-term relationships. An example would be a product manufacturer that tries to recruit new retail chains to carry its products. Often it will have two separate sales forces—one to sign up the retail chains and another to manage the ongoing relationships. The first sales force is pursuing opportunities, because its sellers are engaged in multistage "sales" that proceed from a lead to a close. An Opportunity Management process would suit them just fine. The second sales force is managing accounts, because its sellers are engaged in retaining and growing existing customers. An Account Management process would be appropriate for them. Despite the fact that the first sales force is chasing "accounts," its activities look exactly like a sales force that is chasing individual deals. Here an Opportunity Management process will enable better selling.

Finally, unlike Call Management activities that can often only be conducted for a fraction of a salesperson's calls, sellers frequently have the capacity to apply Opportunity Management activities to all of their deal pursuits. Practically, the level of effort required for opportunity planning is somewhat self-regulated because a seller can only pursue so many deals at once. And the fewer deals she has, the more important Opportunity Management becomes.

Account Management. An Account Management process is used to maximize the long-term value of selected customers. It helps you to align your company's goals with those of your customer and to find compelling ways to strengthen your business relationship. Recall that the key Account Management activities are assessing your customer's needs, aligning your goals with theirs, developing an action plan to create mutual value, and executing the items in the plan. Beyond just planning what you want to *get* from your key customers, a good Account Management process helps you determine what you must give them in return.

So in what situation would an Account Management process be appropriate for a given selling role? That is, who would want to invest an additional level of effort in bolstering certain customer relationships? Obviously, this process would be irrelevant for a salesperson who did not call on existing customers. By definition, Account Management activities are focused on customers with ongoing relationships that lead to repeated purchases over time. Therefore, an Account Management process is relevant if:

> [**The seller pursues multiple opportunities**
> **over time with the same customer.**]

Many salespeople never see a repeat customer. In some cases, their role is defined as such—they are "hunters" who are exclusively focused on acquiring new customers for their companies. If there are additional opportunities to pursue after the initial sale, other sales roles in their organization will take ownership of the account. In other instances, a company may not have the product breadth to up-sell or cross-sell to its customers. Its salespeople make one sale to a prospect and then move on as a practical reality. Either way, these roles would have no use for an Account Management process.

On the other hand, many salespeople engage the same customers again and again in attempts to sell, resell, cross-sell, and up-sell additional products and services into those accounts. Their customers and prospects are the very same targets, and leveraging their existing relationships is their primary go-to-market strategy. In situations like these in which the salesperson's role is to retain and grow an established base of customers, Account Management activities are highly pertinent.

But the fact that a sales role calls on existing customers is not sufficient to justify a full-blown Account Management process. Proactively managing customer relationships requires a meaningful investment on the part of the selling organization. Salespeople can spend days, weeks, or even months developing and executing a robust account plan. Therefore, Account Management activities are only warranted if:

> **There is an economic justification for the additional level of effort.**

Plenty of salespeople call on existing customers but need not engage in formal Account Management processes. A classic example would be a territory sales rep who calls on hundreds of different customers during the course of a year. Each of her individual customers contributes a small amount of economic value, but in sum her territory yields a sizable profit. Sales roles like these target existing customers exclusively, but "managing" their individual relationships would not be worth the incremental effort required. These are efficiency-driven roles, and customer visit frequency takes precedent over customer intimacy.

However, when a salesperson services only a few customers or his profits are highly concentrated in a small number of accounts, it's well worth the investment of resources to ensure that these customers are nurtured and fed. The economic impact of losing an account could be felt across an organization, and the opportunity for growth with these customers is often great. Aligning your company's goals with theirs and paying close attention to the relationship is a wise thing to do. An

Account Management process is the perfect fit for sales roles that find themselves with these types of customers.

Territory Management. A Territory Management process is intended to help salespeople allocate their time most efficiently across a large group of assorted customers and prospects. By forcing sellers to prioritize their customers and execute their call patterns accordingly, this set of activities makes certain that your sales force's effort is directed at your preferred types of customers. Unlike the three previously discussed processes that boost salesperson effectiveness, Territory Management activities help drive organizational efficiency.

What type of sales role, though, would *not* benefit from using a Territory Management process? Couldn't every salesperson profit from more efficient allocation of sales calls? No, not really. Believe it or not, many salespeople are not in control of their calling patterns. Some receive inbound phone calls, and others are given leads on which they follow up. They don't choose when and where to focus their effort, because their effort is focused by design. Therefore, a Territory Management process is only relevant if:

> **The sales role makes proactive outbound sales calls.**

For Territory Management activities to have relevance for a salesperson, she must be in control of her own schedule. If the seller is receiving sales calls rather than proactively making them, then the concept of prioritizing her effort is rendered useless. Or if the person is primarily in a supporting role, such as a subject matter expert, she may be called upon only as needed by the frontline sellers. There are actually plenty of roles in sales forces that are reactive in their stance. For these roles, Territory Management is an unnecessary exercise.

Of course, most salespeople do manage their own schedules and allocate their own effort, so does that mean that every salesperson who is in control of his own calendar should employ Territory Management activities? No, it doesn't. Since

Territory Management is a process for allocating effort, it's only valuable if a salesperson has too little time to fully service all of her assigned accounts. If a rep can comfortably lavish attention on all of her accounts, she wouldn't need to ration her effort. Therefore, Territory Management activities are most relevant if:

> ## The seller is assigned too many customers to fully engage them all.

A major account manager may be responsible for only a handful of customers, or even a single account. If so, she will be able to invest whatever effort is necessary to maximize the value of each customer. However, if a salesperson is assigned 200 accounts, there is an implicit expectation that she will attend to some of those customers with a greater intensity than others. In this case, Territory Management is a necessary endeavor if any of the accounts are to be served sufficiently. Without a deliberate plan for how the seller will allocate her time most appropriately, *all* of the accounts will likely be underserved.

There is one final condition that must be met for a Territory Management process to be most meaningful. At its best, Territory Management is not only about making as many sales calls as possible—it's about making the right types of calls on the prospects and customers with the highest potential value. This, of course, assumes not only that you've identified your high-value customers but also that you want to attend to them disproportionately. Consequently, Territory Management is particularly valuable if:

> ## You want to treat different types of customers differently.

If all of your prospects and customers have equal value in your company's eyes, then a Territory Management process would be an unnecessary level of rigor in forming your call patterns. You wouldn't need to emphasize one group of customers over another, so you could simply design your salespeople's territories such that they have enough time to call on all of their targets with your preferred frequency. Therefore, Territory Management activities are only worthwhile if you want to discriminate among different types of customers and over-allocate your effort toward those that are most desirable.

Sales Force Enablement. Sales Force Enablement activities are intended to increase the sales force's ability to execute the previous four processes. But unlike Call, Opportunity, Account, and Territory Management activities, Sales Force Enablement is a collection of management decisions that are primarily the domain of sales leadership. Whether it pertains to recruiting, organizing, training, coaching, equipping, or assessing salespeople, management must decide how to invest its resources to make the biggest impact on sales force performance.

Also unlike the other sales processes, Sales Force Enablement is compulsory. You don't look at sales management and ask, "Should it be enabling the sales force?" It is unquestionably the role of every sales manager to enable better execution by the sales force. However, the breadth of the Sales Force Enablement activities is great, and responsibilities for each could be distributed across several different roles in an organization, even business functions outside of sales like human resources or finance. So rather than asking in what situation Sales Force Enablement activities would be relevant for your sales force, the real question to ask is:

> **Which roles should be responsible for performing these specific activities?**

We will not attempt to answer this question because it can only be answered in the context of your own organization (see Figure 6.3). Depending on how your company is structured and where the competencies reside, responsibility for these activities could belong directly in your field sales force, in a sales operations group, in another business function, or even with an external partner completely outside of your company. The goal

SALES PROCESS	APPLICABILITY TO AN INDIVIDUAL ROLE
Call Management	The seller makes a low to moderate number of unique sales calls that greatly affect the outcome of the deal.
Opportunity Management	The seller pursues complex, multistage deals.
Account Management	The seller pursues multiple opportunities with the same customer, and additional planning effort is economically justified.
Territory Management	The seller makes proactive sales calls on a large population and must allocate time across different types of customers.
Sales Force Enablement	A person inside or outside of a sales force recruits, organizes, trains, coaches, equips, or assesses salespeople.

FIGURE 6.3

The Relevance of Particular Sales Processes to Different Selling Roles

is to find the *most qualified* resources for the specific Sales Force Enablement activity in question.

If your human resources department doesn't recruit the best salespeople, then don't let it recruit for you. If your corporate training group doesn't have the best sales trainers, then don't let it train. If your sales managers aren't the best coaches, then give us a call. Sales Force Enablement activities are too critical to a sales force's performance to have them reside in a place of convenience. You need to identify the most capable resources to enable your sales force and then point them toward very specific outcomes. With focused effort by best-in-class resources, your sales force's ability to execute its key activities can increase dramatically.

Process-Role Matchmaking

Now that you have your sales roles clearly delineated and some guidelines for which sales processes could be relevant for each, it's time to play matchmaker. As you might have concluded reading

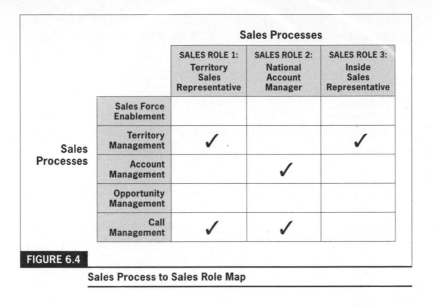

		Sales Processes		
		SALES ROLE 1: Territory Sales Representative	**SALES ROLE 2:** National Account Manager	**SALES ROLE 3:** Inside Sales Representative
Sales Processes	Sales Force Enablement			
	Territory Management	✓		✓
	Account Management		✓	
	Opportunity Management			
	Call Management	✓	✓	

FIGURE 6.4

Sales Process to Sales Role Map

through the preceding paragraphs, picking the right processes for each selling role is not always a straightforward feat. Often, there is more than one process that aligns with a particular salesperson's job description. Unless your sales roles are very narrowly defined (which is not a bad thing), you will find that their daily activities capture elements of multiple sales processes.

For instance, you may have a role in your sales force that is responsible for prospecting within a region (Territory Management) and then pursuing the multistage deals that are uncovered (Opportunity Management). In another case, you may have sellers responsible for servicing dozens of small customers (Territory Management) as well as maintaining a handful of strategic accounts (Account Management). And in either case, the nature of their sales calls may warrant Call Management activities. It's easy to see how a salesperson's day-to-day activities can be reflected in more than one sales process, and you might need to employ more than one process to measure and manage them effectively.

To assess which processes you should have in your own sales force, create a chart like the one in Figure 6.4. This will help you identify your individual selling roles and take inventory of the formal processes that might be relevant to each. This example comes from a past client of ours that we took through a similar exercise.

The most prevalent role in our client's sales force was the territory sales rep, who was responsible for canvassing particular geographic territories. Territory sales reps contacted both small and large customers with varying frequency, and their calls on the larger accounts were highly varied interactions that required careful planning to conduct effectively. Therefore, Territory and Call Management were deemed necessary for this role.

Our client also had a national account manager role who was responsible for growing relationships with large accounts strategically important to the company. The interactions with these accounts took place at very high levels in the customers' organizations, so extensive preparation was required for each sales call. Therefore, Account and Call Management processes were considered highly relevant for this particular role.

Finally, the sales force had inside sales reps that made outbound calls for both prospecting and customer service purposes. With a database of several thousand customers and prospects, it was important for the inside sales reps to focus their attention on their highest-priority targets. Consequently, Territory Management activities were a must. However, the content of the phone calls was typically scripted, so Call Management was less relevant for this role than for the Territory Sales Rep or National Account Manager.

Most people we take through this process-role matchmaking exercise will have one of two reactions. The first reaction is, "Well, it looks like my sales processes are all messed up." For example, a company with identical roles to this client might have implemented a Call Management process across its entire sales force, which would be irrelevant for its inside sales reps. And the client might be missing Territory and Account Management processes, which would hinder its ability to measure and manage its territory and account managers. In cases like these, there's an obvious mismatch between the nature of the selling roles and the sales processes in place.

The second reaction we hear is, "You know, it looks like my sales *roles* are all messed up." This can occur when people realize the complexity of what they are asking their salespeople to do. Regardless of which formal sales processes the company has in place, this matchmaking exercise can reveal the breadth of activities that are designed into individual selling roles. For instance, we know a sales force with a single role that was accountable for generating leads by phone, servicing large numbers of small customers in the field, and managing a group of key strategic partnerships. Examining the role from a process-driven perspective led managers to say, "Wow. We are asking these people to do so much, it's unlikely that they're doing any of it as well as possible. Maybe we should split this job into two or three different roles, so our salespeople can do fewer things with greater focus." To which we responded, "That might be a good idea."

Whether you discover that your sales processes are mis-aligned or your selling roles are ill-defined, it's rare that we find sales forces with perfect harmony between the two. Salespeople's responsibilities and formal sales processes often change over time, so they can slowly drift apart. Given that reality, it's smart to take a periodic look at what your salespeople are actually doing and which processes you have in place to manage them. Again, when the wrong processes are imposed on a sales force, it not only causes a sense of frustration in the field, it causes a lack of control in the war room. Putting the right levers and pulleys in place is a crucial step along the path to proactively managing your sales force's performance.

Too Much of a Good Thing

When you finish mapping your relevant sales processes to your individual selling roles, you may look down to find that a single role *does* have three, four, or all five sales processes selected.[1] In

---

1. Sales managers often have some customer-facing sales responsibilities, so it's possible that a manager could engage in all five selling and management processes.

fact, most roles in your sales force are likely to have multiple processes in play unless you've defined the roles very narrowly. So if you do have complex roles that demand layers of sales process, is it wise or even reasonable to impose such rigor on a sales force? Will too much of a good thing turn your building blocks into a suffocating procedural nightmare? We think not.

Foremost, this matchmaking exercise may have uncovered an opportunity to simplify the roles in your sales force. If your salespeople are being asked to do too much, it's quite possible that they're really doing too little. We were once conducting a public workshop where we asked the attendees to map these processes to their existing roles, and one sales manager declared, "When I get back to the office next week, the first thing I'm going to do is to reassign half of the activities that my salespeople currently have in their job description. I can now see that they need to be focused on executing one sales process to the highest degree rather than half-executing several." Brick-meet-forehead moments like this are more common than you might think, and we expect that most salespeople welcome the simplified life.

Generally speaking, we see a trend toward sales forces having a greater number of more specialized selling roles. Management long ago began to separate "hunters" from "farmers," but the number of boxes on the frontline org chart continues to grow. From industry specialists, to product experts, to sellers who serve niche markets, the roles we find in sales forces are becoming more diverse in nature and more narrow in scope. This not only makes the seller's tasks easier to master, it also reduces the management challenge of hiring, developing, measuring, and compensating complex roles.

However, some selling roles are inherently multifaceted and incapable of being simplified without compromising their efficiency or effectiveness. In these cases, you can attempt to prioritize the relevant processes and eliminate any that aren't critical to the role. You would do this by establishing the strategic importance of each selected process, as well as its impact on your ability to adequately measure and manage those salespeople.

For instance, you may have a role in your sales force that's primarily focused on servicing your largest customers. An Account Management process would be critical. Those same sellers may also maintain a smattering of small accounts that they call on periodically because they've done so historically and it requires relatively little effort. At first glance, Territory Management activities could be desirable for this role—the sellers are allocating their time across different types of customers. But after deeper consideration, you might ascertain that these small accounts matter very little to the bottom line of your company, and the threat of their monopolizing your account managers' time is low. In this instance, you could decide that Territory Management wouldn't be worth the investment of resources, since it would have little impact on your Business Results or your ability to manage the role. Life simplified.

Alas, you will often have roles in your sales force that cannot be simplified by peeling away layers of sales process. Multiple processes may be required in order for sellers to sell productively and for you to manage proactively. In these cases, ignoring Territory Management *would* put your sales force at risk for misallocated effort, neglecting Account Management *would* threaten a large portion of your business, and disregarding Call Management *would* hinder your team's effectiveness. There's little else you can do except to find a way to implement the formal sales processes in the least intrusive fashion.

But there is hope that you and your salespeople can maintain sanity in a process-heavy environment. As a practical reality, each of the sales processes operates with a different cadence and consumes resources in different ways. For example, Call Management activities are most likely a weekly occurrence for sales roles that engage in that process. But Account Management activities are more episodic, commonly revisited quarterly or monthly.[2] And the highly analytic Territory Management tasks of prioritizing customers and designing call patterns can be

---

2. Again, some sales forces view Account Management as an annual event, which can reduce its business impact to the point of insignificance.

performed somewhat infrequently by management, sales operations, or even marketing. All sales processes have implications for the day-to-day activities of a sales force, but they don't all impose day-to-day demands on its time.

We work with many sales forces that have several formal sales processes deployed in the field. It is neither impossible nor impractical to do so once you've determined which sales processes will help you attain your Business Results more predictably and manage your salespeople more productively. When you know which processes need to be in place, the question you face is no longer, Should I implement formal sales processes? The question becomes, How do I implement processes that yield the greatest organizational benefit with the least disruption to my sales force? Then you can set about the task of "rightsizing" your formal sales processes.

RIGHTSIZING YOUR SALES PROCESS

Implementing a new sales process is no trivial affair. To receive the maximum business impact from the new process, you must approach the implementation effort from an overall change-management perspective. It involves more than just directing the sales force to engage in different types of activities—it also requires you to alter the environment in which the activities take place. Management guru W. Edwards Deming is credited with saying that "A bad system will beat a good person every time," and nowhere is this more true than in a sales force. If you don't support your desired behavioral changes with new metrics, tools, and skills to reinforce and measure the change, your sales force will quickly revert to its previous state. Lasting change is hard to affect, and there are substantial organizational costs to properly deploying a formal sales process.

Therefore, it's *critical* to determine how much change is actually needed in order to reap the benefits of the new sales process. If you've selected the right processes for your individual selling roles, all that stands between you and a highly manageable sales force is the right-sized implementation plan. When we see process implementations fail to deliver their anticipated results, it's often because the scope or scale of the change effort was miscalculated by management. Let's examine two ways that formal sales process deployments get botched.

One classic management blunder is to underestimate the amount of change required for a sales force to adopt a new process. Anemic implementation efforts are analogous to pushing your finger into an inflated balloon. The balloon's shape temporarily complies with your wishes, only to return to its original form once you remove the direct pressure. And so goes the sales force. When too little change-management effort is applied to the sales force, it will comfortably return to business as usual at its first opportunity. In fact, salespeople have told us to our faces that their new sales process was just another "flavor of the week" project to be ignored. They declared that if they avoided the process long enough, it would eventually go away. Balloon, meet finger.

Candidly, management often overestimates its ability to direct changes in its sales force. For example, we've known sales leaders to send memos to the field announcing substantial process changes, expecting the new process to be strictly followed by the end of the day. We've also known leadership to distribute new call planning tools during regular sales team meetings, expecting them to be dutifully incorporated into the sales reps' everyday routine. It should come as no surprise that these war room directives failed to take root in the field. Their "change management" efforts yielded zero return on a meager investment.

"Wait a minute," you might be thinking. "Didn't I read earlier in this very book that sales managers *should* be able to direct their sales forces' activities?" Yes, a fundamental tenet of this book is that sales managers *can* direct Sales Activities and change all of the numbers on their war room walls, which is absolutely true. But it requires more than the spoken word to alter deeply ingrained behaviors—it requires a more holistic approach to change management. Sustainable changes in behavior are achieved only if the entire system surrounding the salesperson is designed to support and reinforce the desired behaviors. Otherwise, inertia and lack of focus will outlast the change effort, and it will eventually go away.

Ironically, the second way that management can doom a sales process is to overengineer it. Unlike the first situation in which inadequate investment leads to process abandonment, here we witness change efforts that are overly ambitious and attempt to pull salespeople too far away from their natural selling rhythm. Ideally, any sales process you implement would simply put structure and rigor around the activities that your salespeople should already be doing. When a good sales process is deployed, you will often hear comments like, "Yeah, I already do this, but probably not as well as I could," or "I used to do this all the time, but I kind of got away from it." These comments show that the salespeople see value in the process because it's congruent with the way they actually sell. You may still encounter implementation challenges, but they can be overcome with persistent reinforcement.

More difficult challenges are created when the new process or supporting tools complicate the seller's world beyond what seems reasonable to them. For instance, a salesperson may acknowledge that a Call Management process would help her conduct more effective sales calls, particularly when calling on new prospects. If that's the case, then you would probably succeed in deploying a process with that specific scope. However, the sales force might reject the process entirely if it was expected to complete formal call plans for every single customer interaction. The process would seem burdensome and perhaps legitimately overbearing.

Another example of overengineering that we frequently observe is a super-sized Account Management process. Again, your sales force may agree that it could do a more thorough job of engaging its top accounts and aligning with its customers' objectives. If so, it might welcome an Account Management process that forces just a little more structure and rigor in this area. However, a 20-page account plan that requires salespeople to document everything they know about the account would

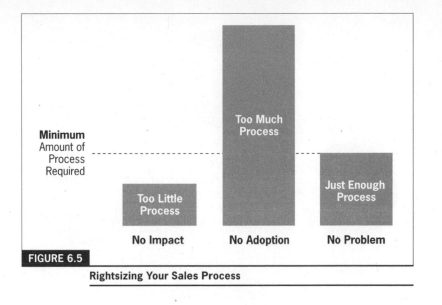

FIGURE 6.5

Rightsizing Your Sales Process

immediately be rejected as a low-value administrative task. And perhaps it would be. If that level of effort is well beyond what sellers perceive as reasonable, then the process will be resented and never usefully adopted.

Of course, we aren't proposing that a sales force's unanimous consent is required for leadership to design and implement a sales process. Many unpopular edicts are still good management decisions. Our point is that it's necessary to find the right level of effort between inadequate change management and process overkill. Either extreme will render an otherwise perfect sales process highly irrelevant to the sales force (see Figure 6.5). It will become yet another flavor-of-the-week project that is ignored until its death.

Our own approach to change management can be best described as comprehensively minimalist. As we just mentioned, we feel very strongly that when you implement a sales "process," you must also consider the comprehensive system in which the salesperson operates (see Figure 6.6). We always begin by considering the strategy—in this case, how the individual role is defined and what it is intended to accomplish within the context of the larger sales force. We then design the process itself,

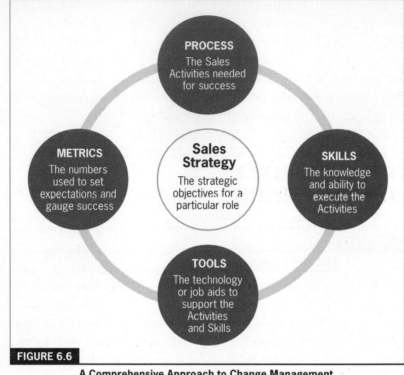

FIGURE 6.6

A Comprehensive Approach to Change Management

which is the collection of key selling activities that must be performed. We then examine the tools that are required to support the sales process, as well as the skills that are needed to successfully execute the activities. Finally, we develop a set of metrics that will enable the effective measurement and management of the process. This holistic approach to change management enables sustainable change through multifaceted design, training, and reinforcement.

While our approach is comprehensive in scope, we try to deploy the minimal amount of rigor required to accomplish the process's objective. The scale of an Account Management process for a sales rep with 10 large customers assigned to him would be dramatically smaller than a situation in which 10 salespeople were assigned to a single account. And the Territory Management demands on a salesperson with 50 medium-sized customers could be much less intense than those on a rep with 500 prospects spanning various industries, geographies, and sizes. Overkill and under-kill are equally as deadly when it comes to change management. If the building blocks of control are too big or too small, anything resting on them is at risk. Rightsizing your sales processes and the related implementation effort is critical to successful sales management.

OFF THE SHELF OR OFF THE MARK?

We mentioned that we are often asked, "Which sales process is best for our company?" With almost equal frequency, we field a similar question: "Which sales process is a best practice?" As you know, our response to the first question is that you don't assign processes to companies—you assign them to individual selling roles. Our answer to the second question is that the best-practice sales process is the one that is right for the role, properly sized, and resides within a system that supports and reinforces it. Probably no surprises there.

But when people pose these two questions to us, they frequently aren't asking us to choose between the Call, Account, Opportunity, Territory, and Sales Force Enablement processes that our research revealed, because not many people have ever viewed sales processes through this lens. More commonly, they are asking our opinion on the various sales methodologies that can be licensed in the marketplace. These are predefined processes that come fully cooked with discrete sales activities baked right in. Need a Call Management process? Got one right here.

Numerous vendors offer off-the-shelf sales processes for purchase, most commonly different flavors of Call, Account, and Opportunity Management. We ourselves have standardized frameworks that we often use as platforms for highly customized implementation efforts. And in fairness to them all, no process, whether off the shelf or built from scratch, is inherently good or bad. The inherent value of any process is completely contextual.

Earlier, we defined a "best practice" sales process as one that

1. is relevant to the role
2. is properly sized
3. resides within a system that supports and reinforces it

It's easy to see where any off-the-shelf process might deviate from this formula. Foremost, the relevance of a process to a role is not necessarily a process vendor's first priority. If the vendor only offers a Call Management process, it's likely that it will try to sell you a Call Management process. And not necessarily because the vendor is dishonest or deceptive—that's just its perspective on the world. If you need such a process, then you are on a path to best practice. But if the sales role in question actually manages a vast geographic territory and makes fairly homogenous calls, a Call Management process would be rejected, and your investment would bear no return. When we find irrelevant processes in place, it's often because of an "I have a hammer, you must be a nail" vendor interaction.

Second, we've never met a one-size-fits-all sales process. The importance of deploying the proper level of rigor in a sales process cannot be overstated, and off-the-shelf processes are commonly engineered to the greatest possible degree. It's not uncommon to find 10-page account plans sitting unused on the shelves of account managers who are tending to 20-plus accounts. There's no way they're going to undertake such an effort for dozens of accounts, and they probably shouldn't. For some sales roles, 10 pages would be just the right amount of account planning effort. For others, 1 or 2 pages might more closely reflect the true need for Account Management rigor. If you've ever been a 2-page variety of account manager forced to complete a 10-page account plan (and we have), then you will appreciate the eagerness with which a salesperson will abandon the process.

Finally, it's extremely difficult to integrate a prepackaged sales process into a complex selling environment. Recall that a process needs to be supported by associated training, tools, and metrics to have any chance at sustainability. Many process vendors will include training and tools that wrap around their specific process, but the alien process/training/tool bundle is usually too detached from the rest of the seller's world to find its place in her day-to-day activities. The process will feel clunky and awkward in the field, and the body will reject the unfamiliar transplant. Of the three conditions that we propose for a best-practice sales process, this is the least likely to be satisfied by an off-the-shelf product.

In brief, off-the-shelf sales processes can be *perfectly* on target with the needs of a particular selling role, sometimes. They can also miss the mark by so much that they are less than worthless—they are a drag on sales force productivity. Whether you choose to build or buy your formal sales processes, you must make sure that they are the right size and shape for your particular roles *and* that they are integrated into a comprehensive change management framework. Only then will you have the right building blocks in place to effectively measure and proactively manage your sales force.

DOES THAT ALSO COME IN GRAY?

There's one final point that we need to make about the nature of sales processes, and it's that there are many different varieties of each. That is, you can buy or build many different types of Call, Opportunity, Account, and Territory Management processes, depending on what your salespeople are trying to accomplish. The key is to understand the underlying methodology of each variation and select the flavor of process that's appropriate to your task. Let us use the Call Management process to illustrate this, since it's one of the most widely used sales processes.

All Call Management processes are intended to accomplish the same thing—to increase the quality of an individual customer interaction. However, salespeople make different types of sales calls, and the particulars of a Call Management process should mirror the particulars of the call that it's being used to improve. For example, the goal of a sales call early in the sales cycle is usually to uncover a customer's needs and motivate him to take action. In these calls, a Call Management methodology that's designed to explore a prospect's situation or build perceived pain would be extremely valuable.

However, once the customer has acknowledged his need and proceeded deeper into the buying process, a Call Management methodology that's focused on exploring needs and building pain becomes irrelevant. A Call Management methodology that emphasizes "gain" would be a better choice, since the seller's task later in the sales cycle is to paint a pretty picture of the prospect's future—not to continue building dissatisfaction and discomfort for the buyer.

An even more specific type of Call Management process would be one that's used to prepare a seller for an upcoming negotiation. The goal of that customer interaction is neither to build pain nor to project gain, but to reach a mutually beneficial agreement on a particular issue like the purchase price or some other characteristic of the deal. In that situation, a Call Management methodology that is designed to help the seller prepare for the give and take of negotiation would be the most valuable framework.

In all three of these examples, we are discussing Call Management processes. One is used to expose pain, one to magnify gain, and another to negotiate the finer points of a deal. Though these distinctions may seem subtle, they can have a huge impact on the potency of your sales process. We've witnessed many salespeople still churning up pain deep into a long sales cycle, just because that's what their Call Management methodology instructed them to do. Conversations like that not only frustrate the seller, they also confuse the buyer. Neither outcome is desirable.

So once you've identified a process that you need for a particular role in your sales force, your process selection venture is not yet complete. You also need to examine the precise selling tasks of the role and find a process methodology that's right for the job. Choosing a sales process is not always a black-and-white decision—every sales process comes in several shades of gray.

As we began to consider how a leader would use the new sales management code to increase control over sales performance, we put a sharp eye on the highly manageable Sales Activities and the five formal processes that encompass them all. These processes are the fundamental building blocks of control over your sales force because they provide your managers with the tactical gears and levers they need to effect behavioral change in the sales force. In the absence of formal sales processes, management's task is reduced to asking for desired Objectives and Results without the means to influence them. With sales processes, managers actually have something to manage.

We then explored the relevance of each sales process to any given sales force and concluded that relevant processes can only be determined by examining the actual activities of individual selling roles. Our insight: the nature of each role determines which processes should be deployed in your sales force. Choosing the right sales process is actually an exercise of matchmaking your individual roles with the five sales processes. This act of selecting the right processes is *the* key step to gaining adoption by your salespeople. See Figure 6.7.

In addition to selecting the right processes for each role, our experience has shown that there are two other conditions for the successful deployment of a formal sales process. One condition is that the process must be sized appropriately for the role. If a process is too rigorous for the day-to-day activities of your salespeople, then it will be ignored and eventually abandoned. If it's too *little* process, then its overall impact will be limited. Therefore, it's wise to ascertain the minimum level of rigor required to enable better measurement and management of the role.

The second condition is that the process must be surrounded by the other components of a holistic change management system if the impact of a new sales process is to be sustained. Notably, the process needs to be supported by the right training, tools, and metrics to integrate the new process into the daily workflow of your salespeople. Otherwise, inertia will pull the sales force's behaviors back into a well-worn rut.

SALES PROCESS	APPLICABILITY TO AN INDIVIDUAL ROLE
Call Management	The seller makes a low to moderate number of unique sales calls that greatly affect the outcome of the deal.
Opportunity Management	The seller pursues complex, multistage deals.
Account Management	The seller pursues multiple opportunities with the same customer, and additional planning effort is economically justified.
Territory Management	The seller makes proactive sales calls on a large population and must allocate time across different types of customers.
Sales Force Enablement	A person inside or outside of a sales force recruits, organizes, trains, coaches, equips, or assesses salespeople.

FIGURE 6.7

The Relevance of Particular Sales Processes to Different Selling Roles

We also shared our observations regarding off-the-shelf sales processes. While they *can* be a perfect fit with little alteration, their prepackaged form can violate our tenets of a best-practice sales process—that is, that they are relevant, right-sized, and supported by complementary components of the overall system. Management discretion is advised when choosing whether to build or buy its formal sales processes. A single miscalculation can lead to disaster.

And finally, we highlighted the fact that not all Call, Opportunity, Account, and Territory Management processes are identical to one another. There are different varieties of each process that are intended to support different tasks. Once you identify that you need a certain process in your sales force, you must further verify that the particular process methodology aligns with your salespeople's needs. Otherwise, your process will produce suboptimal outcomes.

With a comfortable grasp of the building blocks required at the Sales Activity level of our sales management framework, we turned our attention to identifying how you would select and align all of the vital metrics from the top to the bottom of your organization. Business Results and Sales Objectives, here we come.

Selecting and Collecting Your Metrics

CHAPTER 7

IF SALES MANAGEMENT WERE A SNAP

If you have formal sales processes in your sales force, then you're off to a good start as a sales manager. Unlike your peers with no sales processes, you have something to actually manage. But even with the building blocks of control in place, you must determine what you want to accomplish with this potent managerial power. The question for you becomes:

[
Given the ability to influence sales performance, which metrics on the war room wall do you want to change?
]

An underlying theme of this book is that sales management needs focus. With so many metrics and tools at their disposal, managers can find themselves attending to so many diverse things that their attention is spread fearfully thin. Furthermore, the current sales management environment doesn't encourage laser-like focus, because pervasive reporting enables managers to look at their sales forces from every possible angle. If the report is there, chances are they're going to read it.

But what if sales managers *had* to focus? What if they were forced to prioritize among their metrics? What would they do? Which ones would they choose as the critical few? Let us pose an unlikely scenario to see just what might happen.

Pretend for a moment that a team of genies suddenly appeared in sales forces around the world and granted all sales managers the ability to change the metrics on their war room walls by simply snapping their fingers. You would no doubt hear managers snapping so fast and furiously that their fingers would begin to bleed. No metric would be left to chance. This metric . . . that metric . . . and those metrics, too. A frenzy of snapping would surely ensue.

But what if the savvy genies only granted each manager the ability to snap her fingers once? Which single metric on the war room wall would the managers want to change? Ah, that's an easy one. Most would choose Revenue. At least they could be assured that their quotas would be met. Whether Revenue, Profit, or some other measure of corporate health, we'd expect that all wise managers would cut straight to the endgame and snap into effect a plump Business Result. You've gotta love those genies.

But what if those devious genies unexpectedly changed the rules so that the snap could not be used to change any Business Result? Revenue, Profit, and all the obvious numbers are now off limits. Which metric would the managers now want to snap into shape? Most would probably shift their attention to a Sales Objective. That would get them as close as possible to the Business Results they selected before the game's rules were suddenly changed. But which Objective? Should they target certain customers or sell certain products? Should they expand their Market Coverage or increase their Sales Force Capability? Regardless of which metric they chose to change, the managers would be forced to give some serious consideration to which Sales Objective was their best path to their previously chosen Business Result.

But wait! What if those dastardly genies now announced that the single snap could *only* be used to change a Sales Activity metric? No Business Result or Sales Objective could any longer be the finger-snap freebie. Many managers would begin to wonder if that single snap was worth much after all. Though they really want that Business Result at the top of the metrics hierarchy, could they trust that altering a metric at the Sales Activity level would surely move their Sales Objective and nudge a number at the top of the war room wall?

Well, this is actually where sales managers find themselves in the real world—you *can* control your Sales Activity metrics by managing your sales processes. And your reality is even a little better than the nasty genies' final offer, because you can have as many snaps as you like. But how to use those snaps? Which numbers would you want to change at the bottom of the measurement framework to influence your Sales Objectives and achieve your Business Results? How can you be sure that the chain of events will be unbroken? Uncertainty can be crippling.

CHOOSING <u>A</u>CTIVITY, <u>O</u>BJECTIVE, AND <u>R</u>ESULT METRICS

This vignette illustrates why it's so important to know how the numbers on your war room wall work. You need to choose a set of interrelated metrics that credibly link your field-level Sales Activities to the Sales Objectives and Business Results you want. Just like the managers in this fictitious scenario, you should reverse-engineer a set of metrics level by level that will allow you to manage your Activities and then watch the Objective and Result numbers move obediently. You need to have your own causal chain of metrics, which we abbreviate as your A-O-R metrics (Activities, Objectives, and Results). See Figure 7.1.

Of course, selecting your A-O-R metrics is an important task unto itself. If your set of numbers is improperly devised, then the causal chain of events *will* be broken, and you won't be able to manage your sales force with confidence. Without dependable linkages from the bottom to the top of the sales management framework, you can't be certain that your effort will lead to your expected outcomes. Your Activities must drive your Objectives, and your Objectives must lead to your Results.

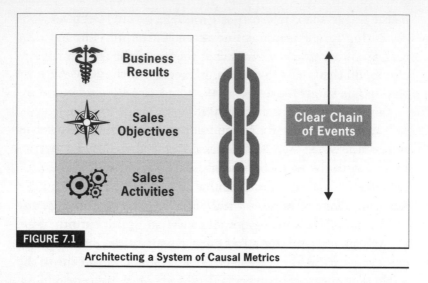

FIGURE 7.1

Architecting a System of Causal Metrics

It's the only way that the newly cracked sales management code can be used to manage your sales force's performance.

We refer to this set of selected metrics as A-O-R rather than R-O-A because it emphasizes Activities as the drivers of the Objectives and Results. In the field, the Activities are what you can directly affect, and there can't be enough attention put on those things that you can actually manage. However, identifying these metrics is a top-down affair, so you actually select your metrics beginning with Business Results. You should always begin with the end in mind, and in this case, the end is your Results. Conveniently, these happen to be the easiest numbers to identify. The Rs are typically selected at very high levels in the organization and then handed down to the sales force as targets. Whatever your company chooses as its highest-level measurements, the Rs are rarely a mystery. Just look in your annual report.

Isolating the Os in your metrics can require a little more deliberation. If your ultimate Business Result happens to be increasing your Revenue, there are lots of potential Objectives that could lead you to that outcome. You could target any of several Customer Focus Objectives, like expanding your Share of Wallet, acquiring new customers, or even entering new markets. Or you could target Product Focus Objectives, like launching a new product line or cross-selling your existing products. *And* either of those changes in strategy might require you to adjust other Objectives, like your Market Coverage or Sales Force Capability.

In any event, the real challenge here is not to merely uncover ways to increase your Revenue. There are countless ways to accomplish that. The challenge is to find the *easiest* way to achieve your Result by choosing the Objectives that have greatest odds for success. For example, if you already have a high Share of Wallet, then it's *possible* that deeper customer penetration could get you where you want to go. But it might be a much smarter strategy to target new prospects where dramatic growth is a more reasonable expectation. On the other hand, if you currently have a high market penetration, then increasing Share of Wallet with your current customers might be a more likely path. Whatever your choice, identifying the right Objectives is an exercise that demands careful consideration of each alternative because not all alternatives are created equal.

Of course, once you've nailed down your highest-impact Sales Objectives, you need to back into the Sales Activities that you'll manage toward those intermediate goals. We mentioned several examples earlier in the book, such as increasing your account planning activities to drive higher Share of Wallet or boosting your Number of Prospects Called to drive new customer acquisition. The breadth of the specific activities you could undertake to achieve an Objective is endless. Here, like when selecting your Os, careful deliberation is encouraged.

At this point in the book, you understand that you must reverse-engineer your path through the management framework, but there's a very important and often overlooked task remaining: to assign quantitative values to your A-O-Rs. For example, if you decide to grow your revenue by acquiring new customers as the result of increased prospecting activity, then you've solved for the *qualitative* half of the formula. However, you also need to determine *how much* revenue from *how many* new customers from *how many* prospecting calls. Without clear targets for your Results, Objectives, and Activities, it's hard to predict whether you'll end up where you want to be. You can do all the right things and still not attain your desired outcomes if you're not doing those things *in the right measure*. Remember the old adage: what gets measured gets done.

BRINGING BACK THE SMILES

To illustrate this in a familiar setting, let's refer back to our old friends Avery and Griffin. During their amazing three-year run that doubled the size of their workplace productivity company, they stated very explicitly the Results, Objectives, and Activities that they expected from their sales force. Recall that their desired Business Result remained the same during that period—to grow Revenue by 25% each year. However, their key Sales Objectives shifted repeatedly, depending on the situation they faced at the time. Every year, they reverse-engineered their A-O-R metrics to keep their sales force focused on the behaviors they wanted in the field.

During the first year of their growth phase, they found that their flagship product, the Smile-a-While, had already penetrated 80% of its target market. Therefore, it was unlikely that they could depend on growth in Smile-a-While sales to double the size of their company. They decided to turn their Product Focus toward their new product line, the Grin-Again, which showed great promise. Not being someone to leave anything to chance, Avery cleverly assigned a value to this new Sales Objective so her management team would keep their eyes on the prize. Their year-one target was to get 30% of the company's revenue from the sale of Grin-Agains.

To shift their Product Focus, they also needed to shift their Market Coverage toward the owners of smaller office buildings, which were the ideal prospects for the Grin-Again. They therefore set a second Objective to contact 25% of all Grin-Again prospects at least once each quarter. And to achieve that level of coverage, they provided guidance at the Activity level as well, requiring each rep to make 10 Grin-Again prospecting calls per

		METRIC	TARGET
⚕	**R**esults	• Revenue Growth	25%
🧭	**O**bjectives	• % of Revenue from Grin-Agains • % of Grin-Again Prospects Contacted per Quarter	30% 25%
⚙	**A**ctivities	• # of Calls on Grin-Again Prospects per Week per Rep	10

FIGURE 7.2

Year-One A-O-R Metrics

week. Their year-one A-O-Rs would have therefore looked like the chart in Figure 7.2.

In year two, their desired Business Result of 25% Revenue Growth remained constant, but their Sales Objectives needed to change. They had achieved their Market Coverage objective, so they needed a new lever to continue their top-line growth. Through analysis, they discovered that their Grin-Again Close Rate was substantially lower than that of the Smile-a-While because a high percentage of their proposals were being rejected. This led them to conclude that their most likely path to higher Grin-Again Revenue in year two was to increase their Sales Force Capability with that product.

They again shifted their focus and set two new Objectives: to close 40% of their Grin-Again opportunities by winning 60% of their Grin-Again proposals. In order to achieve those Objectives, they made a critical change at the Activity level, requiring that all outgoing proposals be reviewed with a sales manager. In year two, then, their new A-O-Rs (in Figure 7.3) would have looked somewhat different.

By year three, Avery had developed a quite capable sales force that was fully deployed against her target markets. How could

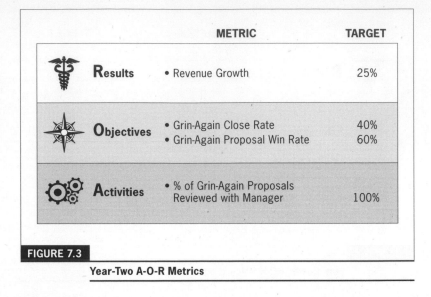

	METRIC	TARGET
Results	• Revenue Growth	25%
Objectives	• Grin-Again Close Rate • Grin-Again Proposal Win Rate	40% 60%
Activities	• % of Grin-Again Proposals Reviewed with Manager	100%

FIGURE 7.3

Year-Two A-O-R Metrics

she continue to achieve her desired Result of 25% Revenue Growth? Since she had played out her most obvious Sales Objectives in years one and two, she needed to find a new path to the top line. Fortunately, one of her sales reps discovered that there was another fertile market for the Grin-Again: school systems.

They quickly changed their Customer Focus and set an Objective to get 30% of year-three Revenue from the education segment. A new year, a new Objective. Avery also made many adjustments to the Activities of the sales force, such as requiring that each rep make a dozen prospecting calls per week. In the final year of the three-year period, their A-O-Rs would have changed once more, as shown in Figure 7.4.

In each case, these numbers were perfectly aligned from top to bottom. Each Activity emphasized was chosen because it would directly influence an Objective that would directly influence a Result. And each Objective and Activity was paired with a quantified target that was calculated by working backward from the ultimate goal of 25% Revenue Growth. If the assumptions that went into these decisions were sound and the managers were persistent, it would take a great external force to keep this

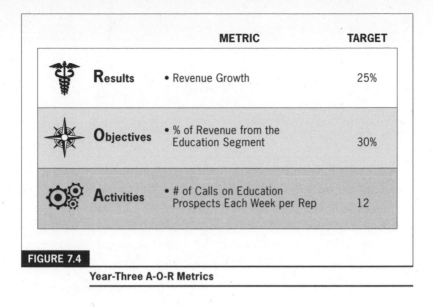

		METRIC	TARGET
Results		• Revenue Growth	25%
Objectives		• % of Revenue from the Education Segment	30%
Activities		• # of Calls on Education Prospects Each Week per Rep	12

FIGURE 7.4

Year-Three A-O-R Metrics

company from achieving its goals. Nothing in life is certain, but engineering a set of metrics like these will bring you as close as you're going to get to predictable sales force performance.

THE SHAPE OF THINGS TO COME

In these examples, we demonstrated a characteristic of the A-O-R metrics architecture that is worthy of mention. Previously, we have only used sets of Activities, Objectives, and Results that were linear in nature—a single Activity drove a single Objective toward a single Result. For instance, increased Account Management leads to increased Share of Wallet leads to greater Market Share. However, things are not so tidy in the real world. When you begin to create your own set of metrics, you'll discover that the linkages are typically more complex than a straight path from the bottom to the top.

In reality, Activities, Objectives, and Results can zig and zag through the framework, with linkages pointing across the same level or even bouncing between them. In the original narrative of the Avery-Griffin tale, the targeted Result for year one was a

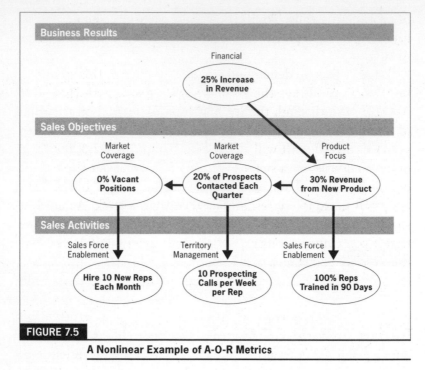

FIGURE 7.5

A Nonlinear Example of A-O-R Metrics

25% increase in Revenue. To accomplish that goal, they chose the Objective of launching a new product line, the Grin-Again. At that point, there was a vertical, one-to-one linkage between the Result and Objective levels.

However, launching the new product necessitated that other Sales Objectives be brought into the fray. First, they needed to target a new type of customer, so they set an Objective for covering a new customer segment. *This* new Objective demanded that they increase their sales force's head count, so they formed yet another Sales Objective, to fill all of their vacant positions. A single Business Result spawned three Sales Objectives, each one supporting the next (see Figure 7.5).

With these three Objectives on the wall, Avery then needed to identify the Sales Activities that she could manage toward them. To launch the new Grin-Again successfully, she needed to train her sales reps on the new product line. To cover the market adequately, she needed each rep to make a certain number of prospecting calls. To fill the vacant positions, she needed to hire new salespeople at a certain rate. Three Objectives, three Activities.

Each Objective demanded its own Activity in this example, but that's not always the case. The particular path that your A-O-Rs take through the framework will depend on the type of change you are attempting to enact and the particulars of your organization. It will rarely be as simple as 1-2-3, but sales management is not a snap. When you do set about the task of defining your A-O-Rs, be mindful that the "shape" of the linkages will more likely resemble a tree than a stick. As always, simplicity is preferred. Just make sure you have the confidence that if you manage your chosen Activities, you will drive all of the desirable outcomes that lie above.

LEARNING TO LET GO

These examples also illustrate a wonderful lesson in shifting a sales force's focus. You'll note that each year sales management reevaluated its strategic intent and redirected its sales force accordingly. In fact, in two of the three years, the company altered its go-to-market strategy significantly, launching a totally new product in year one and targeting a completely new market in year three. The organization exhibited exactly the kind of agility that makes a sales force a strategic asset. When change was needed, it responded quickly and with purpose.

Shifting gears is not necessarily a unique management skill, though. Most companies have the ability to steer in a new direction, and every company must do so from time to time. However, there's one practice Avery and Griffin demonstrated that is difficult for many to endure—letting go of the past.

When companies try to change, they often hang on to the things that got them to that point in time. And performance metrics are easy to keep. Adding a new metric to the war room wall is no challenge whatsoever. If you run out of space, just use a smaller font. So year after year, as go-to-market strategies change, the collection of numbers on the wall gets bigger and bigger. Always bigger, never smaller. That is because of one irrefutable fact:

> **Removing** metrics from the war room wall is extremely difficult to do.

We opened this book by observing how prevalent reporting has become in the age of sales force automation. Just press a button, and hundreds of metrics will gush onto a report. But a theme that we keep reiterating is *focus*. When you add new metrics that are meaningful today but don't remove the metrics that were useful in the past, you send confusing signals to the sales force. You're once again saying, "Do more," when what you really mean to say is, "Do different." "Different" is something salespeople can usually do, but "more" is oftentimes impossible.

Avery was able to steer her sales force so adeptly because she provided her team with very explicit guidance. Each year she communicated what she expected them to deliver *and* in what measure. With the exception of the static revenue target, each year the metrics on the scorecard changed. There were three or four metrics that were always front and center in the sales force's mind because she was able to pull old numbers off the war room wall.

If she had taken the more common approach of piling on the metrics, her sales force would have been given a year-three A-O-R agenda like the one in Figure 7.6. When each manager sat down with his reps to review their performance and plan upcoming activities, do you think they'd discuss the new A-O-R metrics for year three? Definitely. Would they discuss the older metrics from year two? Probably. And the outdated metrics from all the way back to year one? Probably those, too. If the metrics are on the report, then management is saying that they're important numbers to hit. And the sales force *will* try to hit them. All of them. Or alternatively, none of them. Attempting to focus on too many things can lead to a focus on nothing.

We once worked with a client that published 28 different reports to its sales force each month. Twenty-eight. At some point in the distant past there was probably only one. And then

		METRIC	TARGET
Results		• Revenue Growth	25%
Objectives		• % of Revenue from Grin-Agains	30%
		• % of Grin-Again Prospects Contacted per Quarter	25%
		• Grin-Again Close Rate	40%
		• Grin-Again Proposal Win Rate	60%
		• % of Revenue from the Education Segment	30%
Activities		• # of Calls on Grin-Again Prospects per Week per Rep	10
		• % of Grin-Again Proposals Reviewed with Manager	100%
		• # of Calls on Education Prospects Each Week per Rep	12

FIGURE 7.6

Year-Three A-O-Rs . . . Without Letting Go

two. And then three. And then 28. The managers in the field were so overwhelmed with data that many of them became numb to the metrics, even the important ones. As a tool to control the sales force's performance, the metrics had been diluted to the point of uselessness. Letting go of the past is as much a part of management as providing guidance for the future. If you want your sales force to focus, then peel away the historical layers of measurement and put a few critical metrics in the spotlight. Then sales managers can shine.

SPEAKING OF REPORTS . . .

Despite our contention that endless reporting capabilities haven't resulted in much greater control over the numbers on most war room walls, the ability to generate meaningful, timely, and trustworthy data is undeniably critical to effective sales management. Without crisp reporting, it's impossible to do the analysis that's required to identify your A-O-R metrics, and it's equally as impossible to put those numbers in the spotlight. Good reports are good to have.

As you begin to think about bringing your own A-O-R metrics to life, you'll quickly come to a point at which the reporting of the numbers becomes a concern. You might have already deduced that the deeper into our management framework you go—from Results, to Objectives, to Activities—the more difficult it can be to obtain the metrics that you want. More than likely, the facilities are already in place to collect data on Business Results like Financial, Customer Satisfaction, or Market Share numbers because they are high-visibility measures of corporate health. Metrics like those are usually only one "Run Report" button away.

On the other hand, Sales Objective data can be a little more evasive. *Some* of the metrics at that level are reasonably easy to obtain because they are culled from sales data that resides in financial or transactional systems. These are measures of Product Focus and Customer Focus that reveal *what* your sales force sold and *to whom* they sold it.

When a transaction takes place with a customer, it's usually captured in a database somewhere. You just need to find that database.

But as you start to consider Market Coverage and Sales Force Capability, you might want to report data that isn't captured in a transactional database. Many of these metrics involve a human element of some variety, and that presents issues with both collecting and validating the data. For instance, to fully assess your Market Coverage, you might want to examine the percentage of its time your sales force is spending with its customers. For most sales forces, these interactions take place outside of their offices. Therefore, the only way to gather such data is to go out and get it. It's not just sitting around in a database waiting for you to press "Run Report." Through sales force surveys or in-person observations, you'll have to go out of your way to collect such time-and-effort data.

Other "human element" complications arise in certain Sales Force Capability metrics. First, there is information that must be manually entered into a system by the sales force. Examples would be the data that populates sales pipeline reports, such as where an opportunity is in its sales cycle or the projected size of a particular deal. When reps fail to update information or get sloppy with their entries, the reports become suspect. And as we all know, when garbage goes into a system, garbage will come out.

Second, there are Sales Force Capability measures like Increased Skill from Training or Comprehension of Product Information that attempt to quantify salespeople's skills and knowledge. Clearly metrics like these are less concrete than Revenue Growth or Market Share, but they are important management inputs nonetheless.

One difficulty with such measures of "soft skill" is that they are highly dependent on the quality of the instruments that are used to assess the salespeople. We've worked with instruments that we would defend to the death, and we've seen others that we'd like to banish from the planet. Unfortunately, we don't have that power. But however they come to be, these metrics certainly have their place on the war room wall.

As tricky as it can be to report metrics at the Results and Objectives levels, the single most common question we get on reporting is, "How do I measure Sales Activities?" When people pose this question, they are no doubt hoping that we'll disclose some secret strategy for effortlessly assembling detailed reports on salesperson behaviors. Unfortunately, there's no secret. It's exactly as you think, a thorny endeavor.

There are primarily three methods to obtain Sales Activity data, some of which we mentioned earlier. First, you can get the data from the sales force itself, either by surveying it periodically or by having sellers enter information into a system on an ongoing basis. Either technique is exposed to subjectivity and inconsistency, but we have worked with companies whose sales forces were extremely diligent about entering accurate and timely data—extremely diligent.

As you might expect, this diligence didn't occur because the sales force was simply predisposed to entering data into a system. Management set the expectation and enforced compliance. If you walk the halls of these companies, you hear managers saying things like, "If it's not in the system, it didn't happen." And you see metrics in salespeople's incentive compensation plans like Accuracy of CRM Data. And you see metrics on the war room wall like Percentage of Reps Logging into CRM. Again, what gets measured gets done.

A second means to obtain data on Sales Activities is by directly observing the salespeople's behaviors. Literally, we mean watching the sales force perform tasks that are of interest to sales management. If you want to know things like how your reps are executing their sales calls or how they're otherwise conducting themselves in the field, there's no substitute for being there. But beware that this type of "data collection" sales call is different from the joint sales calls that managers typically make with their reps. To collect good data, you must play the role of researcher for the day, observing and noting, but not participating. A hard thing for many managers to do.

The final method for obtaining data on Sales Activities is to gather data in the background on interactions the sales force has with software applications or other types of tools it uses to support its everyday doings. For instance, if your call plans are imbedded in your sales force automation tool, then it's pretty easy to generate a report from the tool on your sales reps' Call Plan Usage. Or if you use an online proposal generation application, then it would be possible to quickly find the Number of Proposals Generated over a certain period of time. Tracking activity in this way is unobtrusive because it requires little extra effort by the sales force, but the types of information you can garner are limited by the tools your sales force uses (see Figure 7.7).

We have two last points to make about reporting. Foremost, not all reports have to be automated. We provided examples of manual data collection, but many companies are wary of exerting too much sales force effort to collect and report information. However, if you need certain data points to effectively

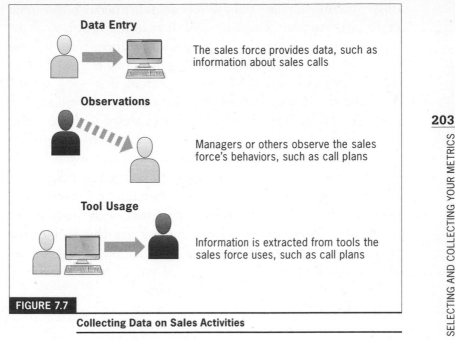

Data Entry

The sales force provides data, such as information about sales calls

Observations

Managers or others observe the sales force's behaviors, such as call plans

Tool Usage

Information is extracted from tools the sales force uses, such as call plans

FIGURE 7.7

Collecting Data on Sales Activities

measure and manage your sales force, then brute force reporting should always be an option.

We once worked with a leadership team that decided it would be incredibly powerful for its account managers to know the profitability of their individual customers. Their internal accounting systems were incapable of generating such reports, because it required the integration of data from several incompatible databases. They therefore hired several accountants to do *nothing* but generate monthly reports on customer profitability, the most brutal of brute-force reporting you could imagine. Many IT directors would cringe at the thought, but it was the most expedient (and perhaps even cost-effective) way to create reports that immediately made a huge impact on the company's profitability. Don't fear manual reporting. Good reports are good to have, regardless of whether they come by pressing a "Run Report" button.

Finally, we think sales force metrics should be reported on a need-to-know basis. It's easy to push reports into the field simply because it's easy to push reports into the field. But when 28 reports land in your in-box Monday morning, it's difficult to know where to begin or what's important. Someone sent the reports, so they're certainly meaningful to somebody. But are they meaningful to you? Maybe?

Not everyone in a sales force needs all available information to do their jobs. They need the metrics that will focus them on their specific Activities, Objectives, and Results and provide feedback on how they're performing. Information overload will paralyze a salesperson or manager and confuse her clarity of task. Once you develop your A-O-R metrics, we'd recommend that you report those metrics and any other information that's required to interpret them—but not much more. Don't turn your salespeople into analysts, swimming in a sea of data trying to find a lifeboat.

STATUS CHECK

When you have sales processes in place, you're in a position to influence the numbers on the war room wall. However, you must focus your efforts on the critical few Sales Activities that will directly affect your Sales Objectives and Business Results. Trying to manage too much is effectively managing too little. You can probably move all of the numbers on the wall if you want, just not at the same time. Focus, focus, focus.

Therefore, you need to reverse-engineer a tidy set of Results, Objectives, Activities, and associated metrics that will most easily and directly lead you to your desired outcomes. As we learned early in our research, this is done by identifying the Results you want, selecting the Objectives that will most directly affect those Results, and then choosing the Activities you can manage that will most directly influence those Objectives. We began to call this focused set of directions the A-O-R metrics in order to emphasize the cause-and-effect relationship between Activities, Objectives, and Results.

Through thoughtful analysis, you can fairly dependably develop A-O-R metrics that will lead you from the battle on the field to the numbers on the war room wall. You just have to take it one layer at a time. But there are a couple of issues we often observe, even in the most deliberate and focused sales organizations.

First, you should change your A-O-R metrics as your go-to-market strategy shifts. From year to year, or even quarter to quarter, you may want to guide your sales force in a different direction, and installing new A-O-Rs in a timely fashion will turn your sales force into a nimble strategic asset in the marketplace. But you *must let go* of the old performance metrics, lest you create confusion in the field. Focus, focus, focus.

Second, it can also be a challenge to collect and report metrics that don't reside conveniently in transactional databases. The deeper into our sales management framework you go, the more difficult it becomes to gather trustworthy data. This is particularly true of Activity-level measurements, which often must be manually entered into a reporting tool. However, if you need the data to manage your sales force, you can find a way to collect it. Otherwise, you are forfeiting control of your sales force for the sake of convenience. Not a good trade.

So with the processes, metrics, and reporting in place, there is only one thing left to do in order to influence the numbers on the wall: begin to manage your salespeople. We now turn our attention to just that—the last mile of road to travel between the place where we began our journey and the place where it will end.

Managing with Processes and Numbers

CHAPTER 8

NOW IT'S TIME TO MANAGE

So now you have formal processes in place with the appropriate tools to support them. You also have carefully selected Activities, Objectives, and Results with associated quantitative targets. You even have crafty reports that shed light on your A-O-R metrics. You've got what you need. Now it's time to manage.

We previously made the claim that the job of the frontline sales manager is the most diverse of any role in a company—part marketer, part CFO, part IT director, part trainer, part coach, and parts of many other functions as well. For our purposes, though, we are concerned with how a sales manager uses metrics to manage his sales reps. Therefore, we're going to take a slender slice of the manager's day and illustrate it in depth. While the other slices are significant pieces of the role, we think that managers can exert the most influence over sales performance during focused interactions with their salespeople.

Recall that not all salespeople are alike. Most organizations have different selling roles that are designed to accomplish different things. Some sellers are charged with mining vast territories for leads, while others are asked to maximize the long-term value of a single account. Some make hundreds of outbound phone calls each month, while others conduct only a few face-to-face meetings a week. The nature of selling roles varies, and so do the activities that each role undertakes.

We also discussed at length how the day-to-day activities of an individual selling role determine which formal sales process they require: different activities, different process. When the right sales process is implemented, it's congruent with the seller's world and allows for the effective measurement and management of her activities. Therefore, within the same sales force, there might be several distinct processes at play across different selling roles.

Why do we need to revisit this point when addressing the role of a sales manager? Because there's a subtle but very powerful implication for a sales manager who oversees different roles with different processes:

> **You must manage different sales processes differently.**

This statement might seem obvious when you read it, but it's a fact that is overlooked by many sales forces. Remember the conversation we shared about the enlightened sales manager whose leadership team was requesting irrelevant sales metrics on the volume of calls his account managers made? *He* understood that different sales roles needed different sales processes and metrics, but his peers and his sales leadership did not. They were busy trying to manage the number of calls that the company's other account managers made. The desire is strong to manage everyone in the same way, because we tend to crave simplicity. But sales management is anything but simple.

And if a sales manager supervises several different roles, then the challenge is multiplied. The manager must measure and manage one sales process for one selling role, and another for another. And potentially another for another. It's easy to understand why managers often fall back on a single management approach. It can get a little hectic trying to manage many processes with an appropriate level of distinction.

Accordingly, the way you would integrate a Sales Objective into an Account Management process will differ from how you'd integrate it into a Call Management process. The fundamental purpose is the same—to provide guidance and measure progress toward the Sales Objective. However, the conversations might vary greatly, one more strategic, and one more tactical. And the supporting tools would undoubtedly differ, one an account plan, and the other a call plan. There are many ways that the management of one process differs from the management of another, so let's then examine how you would practically use A-O-R metrics to manage different types of sales processes.

MANAGING CALL MANAGERS

If you manage a sales role that conducts a low to moderate number of unique, high-impact sales calls, you should probably have a Call Management process in place. Such a process will help your salespeople be more deliberate about how they prepare for and conduct high-risk conversations with prospects and customers. *And* it will provide a venue for managers to coach and develop the skills of their salespeople.

When a sales manager works with a seller to plan for an upcoming sales call, the manager also has the opportunity to ensure that the salesperson's Activities are aligned with the Objectives that are the preferred path to the company's Results. Here is where the management rubber hits the selling road: when a salesperson is preparing to have an actual conversation with the customer and the sales manager directly influences the seller's behavior. From the very beginning of this book, we have alluded to a manager's ability to exert control over sales performance. Let us share an example of that actually happening.

One of our clients had a problem. The company manufactured two distinct product lines to offer its customers, one high-priced premium product and another low-priced basic product. When a sales rep encountered a prospect with sophisticated needs, the buyer would gladly pay the premium price to gain the additional functionality. And when a sales rep encountered a prospect with very basic needs, the buyer would happily accept the less functional product with a much lower price. No problems there.

The problem was that there was a third type of buyer in the marketplace. These buyers wanted midrange functionality at a midrange price, and they could neither use the more basic product nor afford the premium offering. When a sales rep encountered one of these buyers, she had no choice but to discount the price of the premium product or else lose the sale. This discounting put so much pressure on the company's profit margins that it chose to acquire a competitor whose flagship product was perfectly suited to the mid-tier customer. It could sell this "new" product at a mid-tier price point and still defend its profit margins. Ah, sweet relief.

However, this new product could not sell itself. It would have to be sold through the client's existing sales force, so behaviors in the field would have to change. Salespeople could no longer take the easy way out by discounting the high-end product—they would have to learn to sell the midrange offering, which required a push (and an occasional shove) by their sales managers. So to achieve their Result of maintaining a 30% Gross Profit Margin, the company's leadership set an Objective to sell $60 million of the new product in the following year. And to accomplish that, they planned to propose the midrange product in 100% of their sales calls on mid-tier prospects.[1] Consequently, they decided to drive all of this change through their existing Call Management process. See Figure 8.1.

We happened to be working with this company at the time, coaching its sales managers. Therefore, we were able to observe many interactions between the managers and their reps, some of which were good, and some of which were bad. The best ones tended to follow a storyline something like this:

---

1. The actual numbers have been changed in these examples.

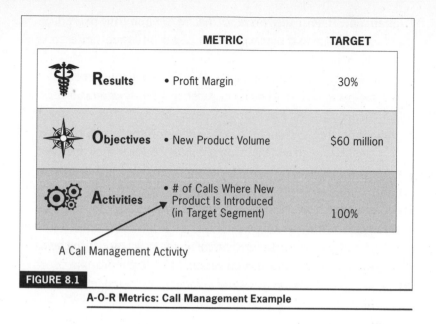

	METRIC	TARGET
Results	• Profit Margin	30%
Objectives	• New Product Volume	$60 million
Activities	• # of Calls Where New Product Is Introduced (in Target Segment)	100%

A Call Management Activity

FIGURE 8.1

A-O-R Metrics: Call Management Example

Sales Manager: *So, Phil, what calls do you have coming up this week?*

Phil: *Well, I have several pretty standard meetings with my existing customers, but there's one prospecting call that'll be particularly interesting. It's probably worth chatting about, in fact.*

Manager: *What kind of company is it?*

Phil: *It's a pretty new player in the market, so I don't think you'd know it. But its operation is pretty similar to Ye Old Company, which I think you do know pretty well.*

Manager: *Sure, Ye Old was a customer of mine way back when I was in your shoes. So what are your objectives for the call?*

Phil: *Well, I've met with its people once before, and they agreed to let me come back to give them a product demonstration. My objectives are, one, to impress them with the demo and, two, to get them to order a small number of units. Once they see how superior our product is, they'll be begging us for more.*

Manager: *Sounds reasonable. So which product are you going to demo for them?*

Phil: *The old standby—our super-expensive, super-functional product line.*

Manager: *Hmm. I seem to recall that Ye Old Company didn't have needs quite that sophisticated. You said they were similar to Ye Old, didn't you?*

Phil: *Yes. You know how it will go. They'll love the product but not the price, so they'll end up negotiating a pretty good deal for themselves. It's a win-win.*

Manager: *Well hold on. We have the new not-so-expensive, not-so-functional product that would probably be perfect for them. Did you consider that?*

Phil: *Sure. But giving them the high-end product at a midrange price is a slam dunk. I'll have them closed by the end of the month.*

Manager: *It may be a slam dunk, but recall our commitments for the year. We've got to sell $60 million in the new product line, and we promised to propose the product to 100% of our mid-sized prospects. How are we going to meet those numbers and get our rewards if we start to veer off course?*

Phil: *Yeah, I get your point. The not-so-expensive product line is probably the best fit, though not the easiest sell.*

Manager: *Then let's spend some time planning how you're going to turn this product into a slam dunk during the call.*

Phil: *Sure thing. Let's do it.*

Conversations like this illustrate how a Call Management process can lead to altered behaviors in the field. They also reveal how powerful metrics are in focusing a sales force. In the absence of a formal Call Management process, this seller would have continued down the path of least resistance and discounted the high-end product. And without A-O-R metrics as guideposts, the manager's argument would not have been so convincing. Processes and metrics are a powerful combination.

Note that Call Management activities are a very tactical affair. Ideally, this manager and rep would go on to plan specific questions to ask, objections to anticipate, and other very detailed actions. If you manage call managers, then you'll appreciate the granularity of this conversation. You have to be prepared and willing to dive into the particulars of a salesperson's sales call and align his behaviors with the outcomes you both want. In a sales force, there are strategies, and then there are tactics.

Call Management is all about aligning the two from a tactical perspective. Let's now examine an Opportunity Management process to see how it differs.

MANAGING OPPORTUNITY MANAGERS

If you manage a sales role that has to navigate complex, multistage sales cycles, then you should probably have an Opportunity Management process in effect. Such a process will help your salespeople examine the competitive landscape, qualify the opportunity, form a strategic approach, engage the necessary resources, and manage a project plan to win the deal. For salespeople who pursue fewer, larger deals, Opportunity Management is often a must-have sales process.

As with Call Management, Opportunity Management activities are an ideal venue for a sales manager to ensure that her seller's Activities are pointed toward her stated Objectives. In addition to improving the seller's chances of winning the opportunities (an Objective of Sales Force Capability), the early stages of a pursuit can also be very powerful in guiding salespeople to the right types of deals (Customer Focus and Product Focus). As we all know, chasing the wrong deals can consume an enormous amount of time and yield frustratingly little return. To illustrate how Opportunity Management can help avoid such wasted effort, let us share an example from a past client.

This particular client didn't necessarily have a problem—it simply wanted to grow its revenues. While working with the client to elevate its sales managers' ability to coach their reps, we made some very interesting observations. First, its sales reps were winning on average about 36% of the deals that they put into their pipelines, which is not too bad considering the number of formidable competitors in their marketplace. But one sales manager's team was winning 70%, *twice* the Close Rate of the rest of the sales force. Even more fascinating, we noted that the average size of his team's pipeline was 25% *smaller* than that of its peers. Finally, his team conducted nearly 50% more prospecting sales calls than the rest of the sales force, and it accordingly produced almost 50% more in revenue. More sales calls, higher Close Rates, more revenue, yet a smaller pipeline. We had to investigate.

We followed this sales manager around for a day in an attempt to isolate the source of his magical pipeline management abilities, and it didn't take long to find the secret sauce. After watching the manager meet with several of his reps to review the opportunities in their pipeline, a pattern of behavior became apparent. The conversations during these meetings were all some version of this:

Superstar Sales Manager: *So, Rachel, tell me what you uncovered this week.*

Rachel: *This week I found three new opportunities that I think are pretty good. Let me walk you through them.*

Manager: *Great.*

Rachel: *The first is with a company we've done business with in the past. We know the key buyers really well, and their current need is right in our product sweet spot. I looked into it, and the company has a solid credit rating and is looking to make this purchase before the end of the quarter. All the stars seem to be aligned on this one.*

Manager: *So you think this is a pretty qualified opportunity then?*

Rachel: *I can't imagine any deal being more qualified than this.*

Manager: *OK, then you should probably go ahead and put it into your pipeline.*

Rachel: *Great. So the next opportunity is a little less defined. We've done business with this company too, but our primary contact there has since left the company. It's definitely in the market to buy, and our products are probably the best suited for it. I just have to vet it a little more. I have a meeting at the company next week to meet the new folks.*

Manager: *OK. Then let's leave that one out of the pipeline until we have more information. Let's revisit it after your meeting.*

Rachel: *Sure. This final lead is also with a company we've done business with, Stay Aweigh, Inc.*

Manager: *Argh. I remember Stay Aweigh. We did something small with it last year. It was a nightmare.*

Rachel: *Yes, I heard about that from someone else. It sounds like it was difficult to deal with.*

Manager: *Oh, it was terrible. Stay Aweigh brought in eight bidders and pitted us against each other for this small piece of business. Then it made us go through two rounds of presentations to reduce it to five and then three competitors. We had to give its buyers sealed bids and everything. We eventually won the deal, but I'd never want to go through that again.*

Rachel: *Wow. I don't think I want to go through that either.*

Manager: *Well, I'm not telling you not to pursue the opportunity, but you'd better see how big the deal is and how many competitors it has at the table. Regardless, please don't put it into the pipeline until you've qualified it a little better.*

Rachel: *No problem. I'll just put the first lead into the system and then wait until I have more info on the other two.*

Manager: *Good job. Let me know what you find out.*

From this dialogue, you can easily see the source of his pipeline management wizardry. Unlike the other managers who were only discussing deals with their reps when they were late in the sales cycle and near closing, he was helping his reps qualify (and more often than not, *dis*qualify) new leads at the *front* end of the sales cycle *before* they went into the CRM tool. By doing so, he was keeping bad deals out of the pipeline entirely, which is why his team's Close Rate was so high. And since his sellers weren't wasting their time taking bad deals too far into the sales cycle, they had time to make more prospecting calls and find more good opportunities to pursue. A simple but significant lesson in pipeline management is to keep out the junk.

With this best practice revealed, the company set into motion some A-O-R–type changes. To achieve positive Revenue Growth, it chose to improve a measure of Sales Force Capability, its 36% Close Rate. It did so by formalizing a new "prospecting meeting" during which each manager would help his reps meticulously qualify all new opportunities *before* they got into the pipeline. This new Activity of qualifying early-stage deals was welcomed by all, and the additional revenue soon followed (see Figure 8.2).

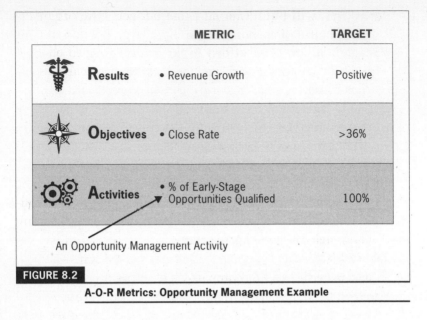

		METRIC	TARGET
Results	• Revenue Growth		Positive
Objectives	• Close Rate		>36%
Activities	• % of Early-Stage Opportunities Qualified		100%

An Opportunity Management Activity

FIGURE 8.2

A-O-R Metrics: Opportunity Management Example

This example illustrates not only the power of good Opportunity Management, but it also highlights the difference between managing call managers and managing opportunity managers. Call Management is extremely tactical, while Opportunity Management is more strategic. It's possible for the same manager to do both. In fact, both are *required* to practice effective pipeline management. However, managers have to toggle their mind-set from strategy to tactics, which is sometimes more difficult than you might expect. Two different processes, two different management tasks.

MANAGING ACCOUNT MANAGERS

Account Management takes the discussion to an even higher level of thinking. Of course, this is only a relevant process if your salespeople are tasked with maximizing the long-term value of important customers. Recall that Account Management activities help salespeople to align their business needs with those of the customer and to engage in the critical activities that will build mutual value between the organizations. If a handful of accounts represent a large portion of your business, then you can't afford to leave anything to chance. Where major customers are concerned, surprises are a very dangerous thing.

Sales managers will then want to be involved in their salespeople's Account Management activities for at least two reasons. First, managers need to make certain their account managers are truly aligning their own needs with those of their customer. It's all too easy for a seller to obsess over what *he* wants from the relationship and to unintentionally ignore the customer's business objectives. In a long-term business relationship, keeping the two companies' agendas in strategic harmony is a mission-critical task.

At the same time, your company still has its own Objectives and Results to achieve. A manager should therefore tune in regularly to ensure that the salesperson is not only aligned with the customer's needs but also that his Activities are driving toward your own company's goals. It's a wonderful strategy to put your customers' interests first, but you'd better have your own in a close-second position.

One of our clients demonstrated an excellent example of good Account Management that's worth sharing. The company's primary business was to provide industrial customers with leasing agreements for heavy equipment like tractors and bulldozers. The company would purchase the equipment directly from the manufacturer and then lease it to its customers for a specified term, typically two to five years. When the lease would expire, the company's sales force would attempt to renew the contract based on the depreciated value of the equipment. A pretty good business, when the price of the equipment and your own financing are in line.

But the company came under pressure to increase its profit margins, so it conducted an in-depth analysis to identify new sources of profitability. It discovered that given current market conditions, it would actually be more profitable if the salespeople could convince their customers to purchase the equipment from them when the lease term expired rather than renewing the lease for an additional two to five years. This was a pretty interesting finding that could make a large near-term impact, since the equipment leases are constantly expiring. Now the client just needed to change the sales force's behaviors to take advantage of the new strategy.

Since the company maintained relationships with very large customers, they already had a very structured Account Management process in place. The sales managers therefore scheduled meetings with their reps to launch this new initiative. The conversations went something like this:

Sales Manager: *So, Anna, you've probably heard about our new strategy for equipment that is coming off-lease.*

Anna: *Yes, I understand that certain types of equipment we're going to want to sell to the customers rather than trying to renew their leases.*

Manager: *That's right. So what we need to do is take a look at all of your accounts to identify which customers have equipment that would qualify for sale and when their leases are due to expire.*

Anna: *Well, let's start with BuildCo. It has about 50 machines under lease, but it looks like only 20 of them are the types of equipment that we'd now want to sell rather than lease. And only 10 of those are coming due within the next six months. The other 10 leases don't expire for another three years. I guess this will be the same for all my accounts. There'll be a subset of their equipment that we'll want to try to sell, and those leases will be expiring at staggered intervals. So I won't be able to just go out and do this all at once. I'll have to plan my approach carefully over time.*

Manager: *Yes, that'll be the case for everyone. It's gonna take some detailed planning so that nothing falls through the cracks.*

Anna: *I tell you what. Let me go through all of my accounts and identify the equipment that we can target to sell in the next 12 months. Then we can review that list together and update whichever account plans need amending.*

Manager: *Good idea. And so you know, we'd like to try and sell 25% of all eligible equipment as it comes off-lease. To do so, I'd suggest that you schedule meetings with your eligible accounts 120 days before their leases are to come due. That should give*

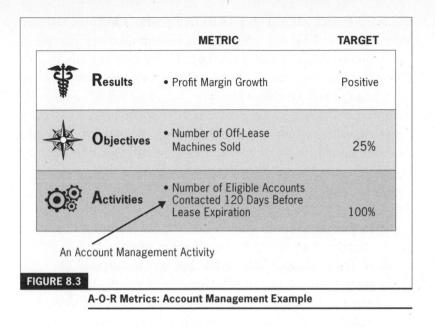

		METRIC	TARGET
☤	**R**esults	• Profit Margin Growth	Positive
🧭	**O**bjectives	• Number of Off-Lease Machines Sold	25%
⚙	**A**ctivities	• Number of Eligible Accounts Contacted 120 Days Before Lease Expiration	100%

An Account Management Activity

FIGURE 8.3

A-O-R Metrics: Account Management Example

you enough time to sell them on the idea and execute all the paperwork.

Anna: *Sounds good. Can we reconvene next week to go through the plans for each account?*

Manager: *Yep. Talk to you then.*

Again, this company was able to quickly shift its strategic direction because it had formal processes in place that enabled proactive management of its sales force (see Figure 8.3). When leadership chose to increase its company's Profits by shifting its Product Focus—basically, selling machines rather than selling leases—it leaned on its Account Management process to create the desired outcomes. If the sales force contacted all of its eligible customers 120 days before their leases expired, it felt that it could predictably sell a certain number of machines, which would in turn boost profitability. And it did. Good management led to good Results.

Note that this interaction between the sales manager and the rep was even further removed from Call Management than the Opportunity Management discussion. This was a conversation at a very strategic level that would help the sales force *uncover* new opportunities that would *ultimately* require call planning, but Account Management activities look further into the future. They are a kind of "meta" discussion that typically takes place with less frequency than Opportunity and Call Management activities. Yet again, we see a different management cadence for a different management task. And yet again, the manager was able to directly influence sales rep behaviors by using specific metrics.

MANAGING TERRITORY MANAGERS

If you manage a sales role that has to allocate its time among different types of prospects or customers, then you should probably have a Territory Management process in place. Such a process will help your salespeople prioritize their targets, design their call patterns, and execute their sales calls in the most efficient fashion. In the world of time-constrained selling, Territory Management can make certain that your sales force's effort is being used in the most highly leveraged way.

We noted before that much of the upfront analysis in a Territory Management process is often performed by resources other than the frontline salesperson—sales managers, sales operations, marketers, or others. But at some point in the process, it becomes the salesperson's job to arrange her travel or call schedule and hit the ground selling. This is when the sales manager should engage to keep the salesperson on the right patch of ground. There are many forces that can drag a salesperson off the recommended path—firefighting, friendships, comfort, or convenience—so the manager needs to help guide the sellers to the right doors.

We have a client that was once a classic Account Management shop. It had historically received more than 80% of its revenue from long-term client relationships, and the other 20% just fell into its waiting arms because of the brand's strength in the marketplace. It had world-class account managers, with all of the processes, tools, metrics, and training in place to predictably retain and grow its customer relationships. Then came a recession.

Suddenly, its major customers were going out of business daily, and its customers that remained were shrinking, not growing. Things were bad and getting worse. Plan A was no longer a sustainable go-to-market strategy. The company needed a good plan B before *its* doors were the ones with locks on them. There was only one thing to do: get more customers.

However, prospecting was not this sales force's thing. Its salespeople were accustomed to visiting their existing customers at regular intervals, and their prospecting skills were rusty—if they ever shined at all. As we now know, when changes in behavior are needed, sales processes are your friend. So this company's management team made a new friend, the Territory Management process.

They implemented a properly rigorous series of activities to identify and prioritize prospective customers, and the leads were distributed to the sales force in a highly systemic manner. They even created Activity-level metrics to watch the prospecting surge from the war room, including a measure that tracked the number of prospecting calls each salesperson made. Everything was in place for a world-class prospecting effort, *except* that their salespeople didn't want to prospect.

Not only was it an unfamiliar activity for the account managers, it wasn't particularly fun. The management team realized that their salespeople weren't exactly suited to the task, but they couldn't replace their entire sales force with master prospectors, nor did they want to. They expected that the economy would eventually return with their Account Management process in tow, so they decided to utilize the key lever for sales force change—the frontline managers. Thus began a series of weekly conversations between the salespeople and their managers that went like this.

Sales Manager: *So Nick, what do you have on the docket this week?*
Nick: (Handing the manager a new spreadsheet with his intended customer visits for the week) *Well, I'm headed downtown this afternoon and tomorrow, and then north of the city on Tuesday.*

I'll hit the other suburbs on Wednesday, Thursday, and Friday. It's a routine that I like to try to follow during the first week of each month.

Manager: *Hmm. The names on this sheet look pretty familiar.*

Nick: *Well, they are. They're my most important customers. I want to see all of them at least once every 30 days, so I usually just go ahead and knock it out at the first of the month.*

Manager: *Well, I'm a little concerned that your Number of Prospecting Calls won't come in where it needs to be at the end of the month. With this new customer acquisition strategy, we really need to pour on the prospecting. Do you think you might need to consider changing your call pattern?*

Nick: *Well, I can't ignore my best customers. Probably 75% of my incentive compensation is on that sheet of paper.*

Manager: *I'm not proposing that you ignore your customers, but we have some pretty specific targets for prospecting calls, as you know—16 each month per rep. And it's a pretty visible number right now. Don't you think you should sprinkle in some prospecting calls this week? Particularly downtown, where the density of targets is so high?*

Nick: *Well, I could, but who would you have me take off that list in your hand?*

Manager: *Well, the question is who would you take off the list to free up some time for an additional day prospecting downtown?*

Nick: *If I had to, I'd take off the smaller customers in the suburbs, but I'll be driving right by them. For instance, when I visit Mega Company on Wednesday, Mini Co. and Micro Inc. are practically across the street. Even though they're not buying a lot from us now, they've been our customers for decades. I think they deserve a 10-minute call.*

Manager: *I can't dispute that, but it's an issue of priority. Our priorities have shifted this year, for obvious reasons, and you'd agree that new customers are the only way we're going to hit our quotas for the foreseeable future.*

Nick: *Yes, I do agree with that. I just feel like I need to get these current customers out of the way before I start making calls on people I don't even know.*

Manager: *OK. Then just help me understand how you're going to make your target of 16 prospecting calls this month if you make no prospecting calls this week.*

Nick: *I'll just have to hunker down and prospect hard for the rest of the month.*

Manager: *That would probably work if you had no unexpected drags on your time, like a shipment coming up short or some other fire to fight.*

Nick: *Well, that's not gonna happen. Something always comes up. (Pause) OK. You're probably right. I'll skip the smaller customers this week and try to spend some more time prospecting downtown. If I get all my 16 calls done early, then I'll visit the smaller customers at the end of the month.*

Manager: *Sounds like a good plan. Then let's talk about who should be your top prospects downtown.*

In this example, the company was trying to defend its Revenue by acquiring new customers. It was an unnatural act for its account managers to suddenly engage in prospecting Activities, but it's what was required to achieve the desired Objective and Result. See Figure 8.4. A Territory Management process became the vehicle for changing sales force behaviors in the field. And again, having quantified A-O-R targets gave managers a mechanism to focus their sellers. In the absence of this process and metrics, the sales force would have stayed on its comfortable course, and the Revenue would have never come. With them, management was able to exert a level of control over their sales performance during a time that it was desperately needed.

AND SALES FORCE ENABLEMENT

Though sales managers don't "manage" Sales Force Enablement in the same way they manage salespeople in the other sales processes, Enablement activities like training provide support to the sales force that greatly influences certain Objectives and Results. Sales Force Enablement activities should therefore be proactively measured and managed

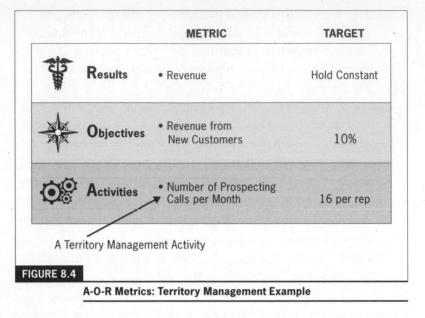

	METRIC	TARGET
Results	• Revenue	Hold Constant
Objectives	• Revenue from New Customers	10%
Activities	• Number of Prospecting Calls per Month	16 per rep

A Territory Management Activity

FIGURE 8.4

A-O-R Metrics: Territory Management Example

in the same fashion as the other sales processes that are more seller-centric.

In our example of Opportunity Management earlier in this chapter, we discussed a company that implemented a new "prospecting meeting" as a mechanism to better qualify deals early in the sales cycle. A savvy reader might have detected not only the new Opportunity Management activity of early stage qualification but also a new Sales Force Enablement activity: an additional coaching interaction between the sellers and their managers. This drove toward the stated Objective of increasing sales rep Close Rates on the way to increased Revenue.

This company's sales leadership of course wanted numbers on its war room wall to ensure that the opportunity-coaching Activities were taking place as planned. And the plan in this case was for every manager to conduct a prospecting meeting with each of his sales reps at least every two weeks. The company then encountered the classic management challenge, collecting dependable Activity-level data on those meetings.

After batting around several manual and automated ways to collect information on the new coaching interaction, company executive eventually decided to deploy a periodic survey to the sales reps. Surveying the sellers would not only allow management to ask whether the meetings were taking place, it would also allow them to inquire about the quality of the coaching they were receiving. They didn't just want their managers coaching their sales reps. They wanted to know that it was valuable to the rep.

And thus, a new Sales Force Enablement metrics was created, though it wouldn't come from their traditional reporting system. Someone would have to "write" it on the wall, but it would be there nonetheless. This demonstrates how powerful metrics can be in not only changing sales reps' behavior but also sales management's.

WHICH PROCESS FOR WHICH OBJECTIVE?

There is one final point that we need to make regarding the use of Sales Processes to influence Sales Objectives. You might have sensed as you walked through the previous examples that some Processes are more suited to accomplish certain Objectives than others. For instance, Call Management is a process perfectly suited to improve your Sales Force Capability, since it will tend to increase Conversion Rates and other metrics that are affected by better selling. However, engaging in Call Management activities—such as planning, conducting, and debriefing sales calls—will not increase your Market Coverage. Call Management is about improving the *quality* of customer interactions, not the quantity.

We sensed these relationships, too, as we originally attempted to define the linkages between the three levels of sales metrics. In the same way that we put "The Question" to each of the metrics at the beginning of our research project, we posed a different question to each of these five processes:

[**Can this process directly affect each Sales Objective?**]

And so it went:

Call Management process. *Can you directly affect the Objective of increased Sales Force Capability? Of course you can. Better Call Management will help move to more deals through the sales pipeline.*

Opportunity Management process. *Can you directly affect the Objective of increased Sales Force Capability? Yes, you can too. This process will unquestionably help salespeople win more deals, since it often helps them successfully shepherd opportunities through the sales cycle.*

Unlike our extended labor with the individual sales metrics, there were thankfully much fewer than 306 questions to ask this time around. However, the questions were equally as difficult to answer in some cases. For instance:

Territory Management process. *Can you directly affect the Objective of increased Sales Force Capability? Well, sure. If you reallocate your sales force's prospecting calls toward more qualified prospects, then sales reps should win more deals. It would seem that smarter Territory Management will drive Sales Force Capability metrics like Conversion Rate. So Territory Management must affect Sales Force Capability. But wait. Steering the sales force toward more receptive prospects is actually affecting the Sales Objective of Customer Focus, not Sales Force Capability. Territory Management won't make the sellers any more capable; it will just put them in front of more susceptible prospects. So Territory Management might indirectly affect Conversion Rates, but only by shifting Customer Focus. Tricky, tricky.*

This is a very important insight as it pertains to influencing sales performance by managing sales processes:

> **To achieve certain Sales Objectives, you have to manage certain sales processes.**

Let's take each Sales Objective in turn and see which processes can be managed in order to influence each of them directly.

Market Coverage

These metrics are intended to show how much selling effort is available to deploy against your targeted customers. Measures of Market Coverage, such as Number of Total Selling Hours or Percentage of Customers Contacted, reveal whether your sales force is capable of covering its territories with a sufficient level of intensity. Clearly those can be directly affected by managing Territory Management activities like adjusting the frequency of your sales reps' calls. Your capacity to cover the market can also be influenced through Sales Force Enablement activities like recruiting and hiring. So both Territory Management and Sales Force Enablement processes are two good candidates to affect Market Coverage.

However, proactively managing your Calls, Opportunities, or Accounts will not increase your Market Coverage. It will make the selling effort more *effective* once you're engaged with a prospect, but it won't enable your sales force to call on any *more* customers. Those three processes are therefore poor candidates for affecting your Market Coverage.

Sales Force Capability

These metrics, on the other hand, are all about the effectiveness of a sales force in getting deals to closure. With this Sales Objective, processes like Call and Opportunity Management will unquestionably help you to move more deals through the pipeline and improve metrics like Close Rates. And Sales Force Enablement activities, such as training and coaching, will also surely boost your salespeople's capability. So Sales Force Capability can be predictably improved by managing your calls and opportunities and by engaging in enablement activities.

Account Management, though, will not necessarily help you advance and close more individual deals. It may help you *uncover* more opportunities in your existing accounts, but it won't increase your chances of winning them once you're engaged. Account Management is focused on the big picture, realizing the greatest value from long-term customer relationships. Territory Management, on the other hand, is about winnowing an overwhelming number of prospects into a manageable group of targets. It helps salespeople focus on those customers that might provide the good deals. Account and Territory Management processes will both help you identify new opportunities, but they won't increase the likelihood of your winning a specific deal. Not a good lever for Sales Force Capability metrics.

Customer Focus

Metrics of Customer Focus shine a light on your sales force's ability to acquire, retain, and grow your ideal customers. As you might expect, Territory Management can be quite useful in this regard, allowing you to direct your salespeople toward the types of prospects you want to acquire. And when it comes to retaining and growing existing customers, Account Management is probably the most powerful process of all. Opportunity Management is even an excellent means to focus your sales force on certain types of customers, because you can use it to qualify (and disqualify) new prospects entering the pipeline. Of course, Sales Force Enablement will help you with this Objective by allowing you to train and equip your salespeople to do all of the above.

The only process that can't help you improve your Customer Focus is Call Management. This is because you never need to engage in Call Management activities until *after* you've made the decision to call on that particular customer. Trying to plan a call in order to focus on a certain type customer would be like trying to plan a trip in order to select a destination. The execution would come before the strategy. Once you select a customer to target, Call Management would be an extremely useful process. But beforehand, it's completely useless.[2]

---

2. You could certainly look at any of the Customer Focus metrics like Number of New Customers Acquired and ask, "Wouldn't making better sales calls help me accomplish all of these things?" The answer would be yes, but only as a result of increasing your Sales Force Capability. Call Management will not help your sales force focus on the right customers.

Product Focus

This final Sales Objective uses metrics to reveal whether the sales force is selling your preferred types of products. As we saw in a previous example, good Call Management can nudge a salesperson to promote a particular product during an upcoming sales call. Opportunity Management can accomplish the very same thing, but during the course of a multistage sales cycle. Account Management activities can also drive sales of preferred products by helping reps form strategies to insert them into existing accounts. And to promote a new product, you might need to conduct product training, which is a mainstay Sales Force Enablement activity.

The only process that is ineffective in focusing your sales force on a specified product is Territory Management. But wait. If you launch a new product that's designed for a unique type of customer, wouldn't redeploying the sales force toward that customer base help you sell the new product? Yes it would. But again, that is *directly* influencing your Customer Focus, not your Product Focus. The two may go hand-in-hand, but simply managing your territory differently will not inherently lead to different product sales. Tricky, tricky. So to accomplish specific Sales Objectives, you should manage certain sales processes. Figure 8.5 summarizes the relationships between the two.

Note that Sale Force Enablement will always be there for you, regardless of which Sales Objective you choose to emphasize. Training, coaching, and equipping your salespeople for success are universally valuable activities. You *do* need to be purposeful, though, to ensure that your enablement activities are in direct support of your current Sales Objectives. For example, training your salespeople to conduct better sales calls might not be the smartest choice if your primary Objective for the year is to target different customers. You might make a bigger impact by training them to manage their territories. So while Sales Force Enablement might always be a good idea, you need to make certain that you've selected the most high-leverage enablement activities for the particular point in time.

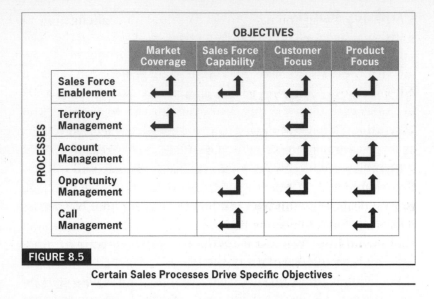

FIGURE 8.5

Certain Sales Processes Drive Specific Objectives

Beyond Sales Force Enablement as a universal lever of sales performance, you need to become a little selective about which processes you choose to manage. For instance, if you want to increase your Market Coverage, then you might also want to lean on your Territory Management process. Or if you want to improve your Sales Force Capability, then you could do so through your Call and Opportunity Management activities. Should you decide to suddenly shift your Customer Focus, then Opportunity, Account, and Territory Management processes would each be potential levers for you to pull. And if your Product Focus needs to change, you could steer your sales force accordingly though your Call, Opportunity, or Account Management activities.

This chart shown in Figure 8.5 is a handy little tool that illustrates the relationships between certain Sales Processes and certain Sales Objectives. After identifying the Objective across the top that you want to influence, you can select a process along the left-hand side that's a viable option for managing that change. It's about as color-by-numbers as sales management gets. It might not be *easy* to achieve your Objective. As we've discussed, change management is hard. But it's no longer a mystery of what you need to do. We'll take a challenge over a mystery every time.

THE TREASURE MAP

We only half-jokingly refer to this Process-Objective matrix as a treasure map for sales management. If the treasure you're seeking is to sell a new product line, then this map will tell you how to find it. And if next year's treasure is to increase your win rate on deals, then this map can point you there, too. No matter what your Sales Objective becomes, there's a direct path to get there from here. You just need to be clear about your destination, and this chart will illuminate the way.

But instead of a treasure map, many executives who see this chart view it as a trail of broken dreams. They look at it and reflect on all of the Sales Objectives they never fully achieved because they weren't pulling on the right levers in their sales force. They'd wanted deeper customer penetration, but their sales force didn't have an Account Management process. Or they'd wanted to get more deals through their pipeline, but they didn't have an Opportunity Management process. They had identified their desired Business Results and even isolated some Sales Objectives. They just didn't take it down to the field level, making them war room generals with no control over the battle.

If you couldn't before, you should now be able to appreciate how these five sales processes are the levers and pulleys to control sales force performance. Depending on which Objective you want to accomplish, there are a few places on this treasure map where you *know* you can apply focused effort to directly influence the outcome. Want greater Market Coverage? You know you have two ways to accomplish it. Want increased Sales Force Capability? You know you have three. More Customer Focus or Product Focus? You have the privilege of four. If there's a will, there are several specific ways.

So this treasure map is the final piece of the sales management code you need to gain control of your sales force's performance. If you want to proactively manage your sales force toward your ultimate goals, then you have a reasonably straight-forward series of tasks to execute:

1. Carefully define the Business Results you want.
2. Identify (through thoughtful analysis) the Sales Objectives that will most easily lead you to those Results.
3. Select a process or processes that can directly influence your Objectives.
4. Choose specific Activities within those processes that you can manage on a day-to-day basis.
5. Make certain that you have quantified targets for all of your chosen Results, Objectives, and Activities.
6. Manage.

Whether you are a chief sales officer or a frontline sales manager, this path to greater control is the same. As a practical reality, you may have to share responsibility for some of these tasks with others across your organization—senior executives, marketers, and others frequently contribute to the selection of an organization's specific Results, Objectives, and Activities. But regardless of who owns the individual tasks, the overall plan is the same. Plan from the top to the bottom, and then manage from the bottom to the top. Finally, this is how you "work" the numbers on your own war room wall.

AN ADVANCED DEGREE: SELECTING A-O-Rs FOR THE INDIVIDUAL SELLER

We will close this chapter with a word about choosing Activity, Objective, and Result metrics for an individual salesperson. A single set of A-O-R metrics can certainly be deployed to an entire sales force, and that is how we've treated them in this book. In a sales force with many people in the same selling role, this is a perfect way to measure and manage their effort. If you want all of your salespeople doing similar things to achieve the same outcomes, there is no better way to set expectations and report progress than to provide a common set of performance metrics.

However, many organizations don't have the luxury of a sales force in which all of their salespeople perform identical tasks. Even within the same role, different salespeople may operate in very different day-to-day environments. In these cases, applying a single set of A-O-R metrics across the sales force may be problematic or even counterproductive. Consequently, A-O-R metrics must often be formulated at the individual level. Let us give you an example from recent a conversation with a client.

We were meeting with the head of sales for a global manufacturer to discuss the sales manager coaching program we were developing for his team. He manages a relatively sophisticated organization that sets clear expectations for its salespeople at both the Result and Objective levels. Its desired Business Result is always the same—Revenue Growth—but it tracks *lots* of Sales Objectives. Among the most prominent are Customer Focus numbers like New Customer Acquisition, Customer Retention, and Share of Wallet, because their customers are fickle and tend to change suppliers. Given the variety of Sales Objectives he had on his war room wall, we were questioning the head of sales about his priorities to determine which Sales Activities our coaching program should emphasize. His response was not uncommon, but it carried with it some substantial implications for his sales managers. He told us this:

> Look, the top priority is to make our Revenue goal. That's how we're all ultimately measured, and that's what the CEO expects me to produce. Now, do I really care if those sales come from a new prospect or an existing customer? Sure, we have targets for that, but the reality is that those particular numbers will vary by territory. Some reps have newer territories with lots of untapped prospects, while others have more mature territories where we're already highly penetrated. It'll have to be up to their sales managers to determine the best strategy for each rep. In order to make their quotas, some will need to target new prospects,

This sales leader's comments will ring true to many reading the passage. The ultimate goal *is* always the Business Result, in this case, Revenue Growth. The Sales Objectives, however, are less strictly enforced, as long as the revenue number materializes throughout the year. But the reason that the Customer Focus Objectives are less important to this sales leader is not because he's indifferent. In fact, he later shared with us a rather strong desire to acquire new customers. The reason the Customer Focus numbers are more fluid for him is that the most realistic path to Revenue Growth varies by rep. The differing customer demographics within each territory demand it. Some reps will succeed by acquiring new customers, while others will need to mine their existing accounts. He therefore leaves it to his managers in the field to identify the best Customer Focus Objectives for their reps.

There's no inherent problem with delegating this strategic decision to the frontline managers, but there *are* some inherent challenges. The first challenge is that each sales manager must do the analysis to decide which Objective makes the most sense for each of his sales reps, to acquire new customers or to increase penetration within their existing accounts. In reality, most of the reps will probably end up choosing to do a little of both, which could potentially lead to a loss of focus. But let's assume for a moment that their sales managers are thoughtful and able to help their salespeople select good, crisp Customer Focus Objectives.

The second challenge is that the managers will need to set quantitative targets for each sales rep's chosen Objective. Again, we'll assume that the sales managers are skilled enough to select proper targets for New Customer Acquisition and increased Share of Wallet, but the managers now have the tedious duty of tracking Customer Focus metrics that vary from rep to rep. This is not an insurmountable task. It simply means that the managers and reps must be diligent about documenting all of their decisions and tracking performance. The real challenges, though, come at the Sales Activity level.

Each sales manager will likely have reps pursuing different Sales Objectives, which means that the reps should probably be managed using different sales processes. For those reps who are pursuing a new customer acquisition strategy, a Territory Management process would be quite useful in helping them target the most high-potential prospects. Allocating their time efficiently across their territories will be critical to success.

On the other hand, those reps who are executing an account penetration strategy should almost certainly employ an Account Management process. This will help them formulate strategies to increase their Share of Wallet with each of their selected accounts. And of course, the manager will need to set specific metrics at the Activity level for both groups of reps.

Allowing the managers and reps to choose their own Sales Objectives has complicated the manager's world substantially. If the company had been able to communicate a single set of A-O-Rs across the sales force, the managers could have focused their effort more easily on making sure that those metrics were met by their reps. However, that wasn't practical, given the variable composition of the salespeople's territories. The responsibility for selecting the right Objectives and Activities to accomplish the stated Result fell to the frontline sales managers.

You'll probably recognize that this is not an unusual scenario. Executives frequently set company-wide financial targets and then leave it to the field to identify the best Objectives and Activities to get there. Doing so can lead to a menagerie of go-to-market strategies that causes the lack of focus that this book is intended to eradicate. However, it's not necessarily undesirable to have managers in charge of their own A-O-R metrics.

Allowing A-O-R metrics to be developed in the field can actually be a smart management strategy. In companies like the one we just described, giving this responsibility to the managers will ensure that each sales rep has a set of metrics that's both relevant and achievable. Metrics that are *ir*relevant and *un*achievable are highly de-motivating, so there's a strong appeal to selecting the metrics as close to the ground as possible. But there is one large caveat to this strategy:

> **The sales managers must be *highly* skilled with the A-O-R framework.**

When sales managers are skilled in the theory and practice of A-O-Rs, they are able to set distinct sets of metrics at the individual level that remain in alignment with your higher-order organizational goals. What's wanted at the top of the organization is adeptly driven from the bottom. But when managers are not as skilled in using metrics to manage, the sales force can veer off course by design and abandon its strategic focus, which is not what you want to see if you're the one standing in the war room.

But sacrificing uniformity across the sales force for the sake of local management is often a good trade. In companies that have a clear understanding of the organization's overall goals *and* whose sales managers know how to use metrics to manage their reps' Activities toward those goals, managers become an even more powerful lever for improved sales performance. They have the ability to guide their salespeople purposefully and then course-correct when the market signals trouble. There's little (if anything) in a sales force that is more magnificent than a talented sales manager, unless it's an entire team of them.

So whether you select a single set of A-O-R metrics for your whole sales force or you empower your managers to steer for themselves, developing the skills and knowledge to keep your organization in alignment is key. We've all known sales forces that lacked management rigor, and the battlefield is not a safe place for them to be. A sales force that has a good battle plan and knows how to execute will be victorious every time, and a tight framework of metrics that drives the right behaviors is the best battle plan we know. Teach your sales force to manage with metrics, and the world will be yours for the taking.

As we neared the end of our journey, we began to consider how front-line sales managers would actually manage their salespeople using the processes and metrics our research revealed. As we asserted earlier, a sales manager's role is incredibly diverse, so there are probably countless ways that the concepts in this book could affect them. However, we chose to shine a light on what we believe is the most high-impact part of a manager's job—conducting purposeful conversations with her sales reps.

Recalling that each selling role must employ a sales process that's relevant to its unique Sales Activities, we chose to examine the management task by sales process. It became apparent that the nature of these manager-seller conversations should vary depending on the particular process that the manager is trying to manage. For example, if your reps engage primarily in Call Management activities, then you will integrate your A-O-R metrics into the context of their call planning. But if other reps engage in Account Management activities, then you'll incorporate those metrics into a more strategic account planning session. Each process is distinct from the other, and the manner in which you use metrics to influence your salespeople's behaviors will differ accordingly.

We also discovered that certain sales processes are capable of influencing certain Sales Objectives. For instance, a Territory Management process is perfectly suited to help you influence an Objective like Customer Focus, but it's useless in affecting measures of Sales Force Capability. And while Opportunity Management activities *are* great for increasing Sales Force Capability, they will not make an impact on your Market Coverage. Therefore, depending on which Sales Objectives you are trying to achieve, you must manage toward them by directing a relevant sales process. Trying to achieve a Sales Objective by managing the wrong process will be a frustrating waste of effort.

Finally, we discussed the practicality of allowing the field sellers to select their own A-O-R metrics. A theme of this book is that leadership can gain more control over sales performance by providing clear guidance on the Activities, Objectives, and Results that it expects. However, there are sales forces for which variability in local demographics makes uniform management a suboptimal approach. In situations like this, it's perfectly acceptable to let frontline managers customize their salespeople's metrics, *but* you must make certain that your managers are skilled enough with the A-O-R framework to keep all of their sellers pointed toward the organization's overall goals. Otherwise, the sales force will degenerate from a focused strategic weapon into a collection of individuals executing their own go-to-market strategies, which is probably not what you want.

Mission Accomplished

CHAPTER 9

IN REFLECTION

As we prepared to write this book, we looked back at the many iterations of analyses and frameworks we had developed en route to the content you've just read. In reflection, it was truly difficult to crack the sales management code. This is partly because we were handed some early red herrings but mostly because it was just plain hard—much harder, in fact, than we had expected it to be.

We naively began the effort thinking that it would be a survey of existing best practices. If we studied the measurement strategies of large, evolved sales forces, *surely* the code would reveal itself. But we quickly discovered that even the most sophisticated organizations had not found an intuitive way to organize their sales metrics. Though there were many common metrics across the companies we surveyed, they were arranged as randomly as a dropped box of toothpicks. Numbers here, numbers there, numbers everywhere. It was sales metric chaos.

More discouraging, none of the different approaches to sales force measurement seemed to provide a useful framework for *management*. There was no sense of hierarchy or cause-and-effect relationships that would imply a deliberate approach to "managing" the numbers. There were simply various collections of metrics that were of interest to somebody for some reason. In short, our quick survey of sales measurement best practices was not as revealing as we had hoped. In the absence of any clear best practices, we decided that we'd have to chart our own course through the metrics morass. So the dozens of reports on our wall exploded into 306 individual data points just waiting for a guiding hand.

The guiding hand was, of course, The Question, Can we "manage" this metric? Wrestling with this question brought us to our first real breakthrough, separating Sales Objectives from Sales Activities. But there were more challenges to come. Next, the sales pipeline metrics nearly put us in the grave. Then the compound metrics. Then mapping Activities to processes. Then assigning processes to roles. Then linking processes to Objectives. At every turn, there was some complexity that forced us to walk away for a few days, clear our heads, and then return with a fresh perspective. Two steps forward, one step back. And sometimes two or three steps back.

But here we are. Our work is done. The code is cracked, and the first set of operating instructions for the sales force has been written. We now know that we can predictably control sales performance by directly managing Sales Activities, which influence Sales Objectives, which drive Business Results. The key is to determine the causal chain of Activities and Objectives that will lead you most surely to your desired Results. Where there was once chaos on our war room wall, there is now a refreshing sense of order. Finally, our mission had been accomplished.

THE ULTIMATE STATUS CHECK

After such prolonged and bloody battle with a bunch of numbers on a conference room wall, we think anyone would feel compelled to put the victory in perspective. Did we win a major war or merely a tiny skirmish? What does the world know *now* that it didn't know 306 random metrics ago? Or stated more bluntly, what did we really accomplish?

> **We connected sales force activities to organizational results.**

At first glance, this statement makes the contribution seem unremarkable. Salespeople have been engaged in "activities" more than a century, while organizations have been recognizing "results" for even longer. And we've always inherently known that there is a connection between the two. Is it really a big deal to have deciphered the relationship between activities and results? We think so, and we'll provide you with a final story to illustrate why.

One of our current clients is a very successful global company. It dominates almost all of its markets, and it has dominated many of them for more than a hundred years. The company is routinely found on the "most admired" lists of global organizations, largely because of its commitment to developing world-class management. Its managers are very smart and focused, and they run every aspect of their business with great rigor, including their sales forces. We tell you this to make the point that they don't miss the obvious things. If they find that something is broken, they will deploy a team of experts to fix it. Fast. Continuous improvement is in their blood, and known problems don't exist for long.

During the course of a recent project, we interviewed our client's senior leaders to understand where they perceived there to be the biggest opportunities for improvement in their sales manager's capabilities. We concluded each interview with a straightforward, open-ended question: what skills would you most like to see improved in your sales managers? Here are literal, word-for-word responses from several conversations our team had over the past few weeks:

- "Our managers need to do a better job of linking the activities of their salespeople to our overall organizational goals."
- "They need to be better at managing the right activities."

- "My managers need to help their salespeople focus on the things that matter."
- "They need to be better about focusing salespeople on the critical few things they can do to impact results."

From these quotes, it's clear that this company's leadership recognizes the fact that its salespeople's activities drive its organization's results. It's also clear that it expects its managers to focus their sellers on the *right* activities to attain those results. Company executives don't want their managers to simply scream "Charge!" and then push their salespeople to work harder. They expect them to skillfully direct the action on the battlefield. They expect them to be proactive sales managers.

Obviously, they wanted their managers to do the exact thing that this book describes: direct the Sales Activities that will predictably produce their Business Results. But they weren't doing it. They weren't guiding their salespeople's activities surely toward their organizational goals. And it was such a significant problem that several different leaders named it as their managers' biggest skill deficit. For a company such as this, it was a pretty persistent point of failure.

So why would a company full of smart, motivated problem solvers tolerate this glaring and widespread issue with its sales managers? There's only one reason: it didn't know how to fix it. If it did, it would have long ago incorporated that knowledge into its sales manager training programs. It would have fixed the problem fast and forever. But instead, it remained an obvious problem without a known solution. The company's leadership didn't know how to teach their managers to connect specific activities to desired results because the body of knowledge didn't exist.

This is not the only time we've heard leaders complain about their sales force's inability to connect field-level activities to overall outcomes—it's just the most recent. This problem is prevalent, and we suspect that you've heard similar comments in your own organization. If you haven't, then perhaps you've heard the same grievance stated differently. Executives often complain about this disconnect from their own perspective rather than the field's. They say things like, "The sales force isn't executing our strategy," or, "Our lack of sales execution is a real problem." Whether it's linking activities to results or linking results to execution, it's the same underlying problem—an inability to coherently link sales force activities to organizational results.

This is what our research contributes to the sales management discipline: the knowledge of how to connect organizational strategy to sales force tactics. Our time spent shuffling metrics around our war room wall revealed the levers and pulleys that now allow sales managers to do exactly what they've been asked to do for decades—to focus their salespeople on the few critical activities that will lead to their desired results. Our smart, motivated client now *does* know how to solve its problem, because we helped it incorporate the concepts in this book into its global sales manager training program. Activities → Objectives → Results. A simple yet profound equation.

AND FINALLY . . .

We have an acquaintance who used to be a partner in a global strategy consulting firm. Despite a long and successful career in management, he once confided to us that he had never read a single management book from beginning to end. He said that most business books only contained a couple of key concepts that he could pick up in the first few chapters, and reading any further was a waste of his time. We don't *necessarily* agree, but his point was taken. It's a large commitment of time for an executive to read a book. To justify the effort, the book had better be good.

If you've read this book from beginning to end, then we are flattered. It means that you've judged the content to be worth the investment of your time. We hope that you realize a great return on that investment, and we look forward to providing you with more insights in the future. There's much more to be written about sales management, and we are committed to help write it. Until that time, good luck in the war room.

Appendix: Troubleshooting Guide

PROBLEM	Answer Can Be Found . . .	
	CHAPTER	PAGE(S)
CRM has not lived up to expectations	1	6
Increased reporting has not led to increased sales performance	1	6
Star salespeople fail as sales managers	2	13
Salespeople's training doesn't have the desired impact on performance	2	15
Struggling to improve key performance metrics	2	21
Not meeting forecasted business results	2	30
Low customer satisfaction	3	51
Not getting the overall results you're requesting	3	56
Salespeople aren't focused on the company's key objectives	4	69
Difficulty judging the quality of the sales force	4	90
Uncoordinated selling effort or murky sales processes	5	103
Low-quality call planning	5	111
Too many unqualified opportunities in the sales pipeline	5	112
Challenges in managing the sales pipeline	5	117

PROBLEM	Answer Can Be Found . . .	
	CHAPTER	PAGE(S)
Account planning is a low-value, administrative process	5	123
Salespeople are targeting the wrong customers	5	126
Salespeople are doing too much "firefighting"	5	131
Sales force improvement efforts failed to succeed	5	138
Sales processes are missing or misaligned	6	151
Challenges in managing several different types of selling roles	6	158, 207
Need to select the right sales process or methodology	6	159
Salespeople's roles are too complex	6	173
A formal sales process is too burdensome	6	176
An "off-the-shelf" sales process doesn't fit the way you sell	6	181
Choosing the right performance metrics	7	189
Too many sales metrics or reports	7	197
Collecting field-level data	7	199
Aligning sales rep behaviors with company objectives	8	207
Focusing managers' effort on their most critical tasks	8	225
Setting clear, quantifiable expectations for individual behaviors	8	232

Index

About the Authors

Jason Jordan is a partner of Vantage Point Performance, Inc., a leading sales management training and development firm. He is a recognized thought leader in the domain of business-to-business selling and conducts ongoing research into management best practices in hiring, developing, measuring, and managing world-class sales organizations. Jason's extensive research into sales performance metrics led to the original breakthrough insights in *Cracking the Sales Management Code*.

For 15 years, Jason has worked internationally in industries such as technology, manufacturing, distribution, financial services, construction, media, telecommunications, consumer products, health care, and hospitality. As a popular speaker and writer, he is a frequent contributor to the Sales Management Association, the American Society for Training and Development, *Selling Power*, *Sales & Marketing Management*, and other industry groups.

Having sold financial products, consumer products, and software integration services early in his career, Jason is a passionate advocate of both the sales profession and the evolution of sales management into a science. He is currently the Director of Research for the Sales Education Foundation and is a visiting faculty member in the Executive Education and MBA programs at the University of Virginia's Darden School of Business.

Jason received an economics degree with honors from Duke University and an MBA from the University of Virginia. He and his family currently reside in Charlottesville, Virginia. Jason may be reached at JJordan@VantagePointPerformance.com.

Michelle Vazzana is a partner at Vantage Point Performance, Inc., the most innovative sales management training and development firm in the marketplace today. Michelle is a seasoned practitioner in the sales management arena and has coached and developed hundreds of sales managers and leaders since her foray into consulting more than 12 years ago.

She has broken new ground in the area of sales and sales management effectiveness, helping managers focus on the vital few activities that drive true sales improvement. Her experience in coaching and training sales managers in Fortune 500 companies has propelled Vantage Point Performance's groundbreaking research into practical application for sales managers worldwide.

Michelle is a recognized expert in the area of sales management and sales coaching, and she is a sought-after speaker for organizations including the American Society for Training and Development and the Sales Management Association. She has been the driving force behind the development of Vantage Point Performance's key training programs and leads the firm's deployment of high-impact client engagements.

For 26 years, Michelle has been in sales roles including direct sales, management, training, and consulting. She started her career selling for IBM and Xerox, where she held a variety of sales and management roles. Michelle has worked with Neil Rackham and other thought leaders in the industry to design and deploy pioneering sales performance improvement strategies.

As a voracious learner, Michelle continues to pursue graduate studies in Organizational Psychology to deepen her insights into the interplay between human behavior and sales performance. She has a master's degree in management for organizational effectiveness, as well as master's certificates in Total Quality Management and Instructional Systems Design from Marymount University in Arlington, Virginia. She also has a bachelor of science degree in Computer Science from Florida International University.

Michelle and her family currently reside in Ashburn, Virginia. Michelle may be reached at mvazzana@ VantagePointPerformance.com.